Voyager

Reading and Writing for Today's Adults

6

Judith Gallagher

Advisers to the Series

Mary Dunn Siedow
Director
North Carolina Literacy Resource Center
Raleigh, NC

Linda Thistlethwaite
Associate Director
The Central Illinois Adult Education Service Center
Western Illinois University
Macomb, IL

Reviewer

Linnea Emami
Instructor, Adult Basic Education
Fresno Adult School
Fresno, CA

New Readers Press

Acknowledgments

Anderson, Sherwood, "The Corn Planting." Reprinted by permission of Harold Ober Associates, Incorporated. Copyright © 1934 by Eleanor Anderson. Renewed 1961 by Eleanor Copenhaver Anderson.

Buchsbaum, Herbert. From "Extraordinary People," SCHOLASTIC UPDATE, December 3, 1993, Vol. 126, No. 7, pp. 6–9. Copyright © 1993 by Scholastic Inc. Reprinted by permission.

Darrach, Brad, and Dianna Waggoner. "A Success as a Teacher and a Builder, John Corcoran Had a Humiliating Secret: He Couldn't Read or Write" by Brad Darrach and Dianna Waggoner, PEOPLE Magazine, December 5, 1988. © 1988 People Weekly/Time, Inc. Reprinted by permission.

Delgado, Luis. Adapted from "The Fifth Time." Permission granted by Luis Delgado, a successful participant at the Center for Alternative Sentencing and Employment Services, Inc. (CASES).

Fondation, Larry. "Deportation at Breakfast" by Larry Fondation. Reprinted from UNSCHEDULED DEPARTURES, ed. Greg Boyd, Asylum Arts, 1991 by permission.

Garrett, George from "The Right Thing to Do at the Time." Reprinted by permission of the author.

King, Jr., Martin Luther, "I Have a Dream." Excerpted by arrangement with The Heirs to the Estate of Martin Luther King, Jr., c/o Joan Daves Agency as agent for the proprietor. Copyright 1963 by Martin Luther King, Jr., copyright renewed 1991 by Coretta Scott King.

Machin, Carmen. Student Essay by Carmen Machin as published in PATTERNS PLUS: A SHORT PROSE READER WITH ARGUMENTATION, Fifth Edition, by Mary Lou Conlin. Copyright © 1995 by Houghton Mifflin Company. Reprinted with permission.

Marlette, Doug. Cartoon from IN YOUR FACE by Doug Marlette. Copyright © 1991 by Doug Marlette. Reprinted by permission of Houghton Mifflin Company. All rights reserved.

Pesante, Zoraida. From "A Fear I Had" by Zoraida Pesante. © Zoraida Pesante "Zee" 1994. Reprinted by permission of the author.

Thompson, Ernest. From ON GOLDEN POND by Ernest Thompson. Copyright, 1979, by Ernest Thompson. Reprinted by permission of the author and Graham Agency, New York. CAUTION: Professionals and amateurs are hereby warned that ON GOLDEN POND is subject to a royalty. It is fully protected under the copyright laws of the United States of America, and of all countries covered by the International Copyright Union (including Canada and the British Commonwealth), and of all countries covered by the Pan-American Copyright convention and the Universal Copyright Convention, and of all countries with which the United States has reciprocal copyright relations. All rights, including professional, amateur, motion picture, recitation, lecturing, public reading, radio broadcasting, television, audio and video recording, and the rights of translation into foreign languages, are strictly reserved. Particular emphasis is laid upon the question of readings, permission for which must be secured from the author's agent in writing. All inquiries concerning rights should be addressed to Graham Agency, 311 West 43rd Street, New York, NY 10036.

Voyager™
ISBN 1-56420-156-2
Copyright © 1999
New Readers Press
U.S. Publishing Division of Laubach Literacy International
Box 131, Syracuse, New York 13210-0131

Printed in the United States of America

Director of Acquisitions and Development: Christina Jagger
Content Editor: Mary Hutchison
Developer: Learning Unlimited, Oak Park, IL
Developmental Editor: Karen Herzoff
Contributing Writer: Betsy Rubin
Production Director: Jennifer Lohr
Photography: David Revette Photography, Inc.
Copy Editor: Jeanna H. Walsh
Cover Designer: Gerald Russell
Designer: Kimbrly Koennecke
Artist/Illustrator: Linda Tiff

Contents

Introduction

Welcome to New Readers Press's *Voyager 6.* In this book, you will build your reading, writing, listening, and speaking skills. You will improve your understanding of what you read. You will work with familiar types of reading selections, such as stories, articles, speeches, and plays. You will also work with everyday forms, documents, and graphics.

This book has four units. Each unit is based on a theme that reflects our day-to-day lives. In *Voyager 6,* you will be exploring these themes:
- ▶ Success at Work
- ▶ Taking a Stand
- ▶ Relationships
- ▶ Insights

Within each theme-based unit, you will find three lessons. Each lesson has the following features:
- ▶ **Before You Read:** a strategy to help you understand what you read
- ▶ **Reading:** a story, article, biography, autobiography, speech, play, or other type of reading
- ▶ **After You Read:** questions and activities about the reading
- ▶ **Think About It:** a reading skill that will help you understand what you read
- ▶ **Write About It:** an activity to improve your writing skills
- ▶ **Life Skill:** an activity to help you understand and interpret real-life reading material

We hope you enjoy exploring the themes and mastering the skills found in *Voyager 6.* We also invite you to continue your studies with the next book in our series, *Voyager 7.*

Student Self-Assessment #1

Before you begin the Skills Preview, do this self-assessment. Share your responses with your instructor.

Reading	Good at this	Need help	Don't know how to do this
I can read and understand			
1. stories, poems, biographies, fables, and essays			
2. articles in magazines, newspapers, books, and letters			
3. paycheck stubs, forms, and applications			
4. charts, graphs, diagrams, maps, and time lines			
5. political cartoons			
When I read, I can			
1. figure out new words by using context clues			
2. empathize with characters in a story			
3. use what I already know to help me understand			
4. skim to get a general idea of the reading material			
5. try to predict what is coming next			
6. visualize what I read			
7. identify cause and effect relationships			
8. identify facts and opinions			
9. identify the main idea, details, and theme			
10. compare and contrast information			
11. make inferences about information not stated			
12. summarize what I've read			

Writing	Good at this	Need help	Don't know how to do this
I can fill in or write			
1. paragraphs with a topic sentence and supporting details			
2. forms and applications			
3. business and friendly letters			
4. stories and biographical sketches			
5. my opinion on an issue			
6. dialogue			
7. an article based on comparisons and contrasts			
8. an article based on cause and effect			
When I write, I can			
1. think of good ideas			
2. organize my ideas			
3. use facts, examples, or reasons to support my main ideas			
4. express myself clearly so others understand			
5. revise my writing to improve it			
6. edit my writing to make subjects and verbs agree			
7. write and punctuate compound and complex sentences correctly			
8. use the correct forms of pronouns			

Skills Preview

This preview will give you an idea of the kinds of readings and skills covered in this book. Before you begin Unit 1, please complete the entire preview. Then share your work with your instructor.

Reading Skills Preview

Read each passage and answer the questions that follow.

When Love Is Not Enough

Most people know that falling-in-love feeling. Two people want to be together all the time. They feel that they don't need anyone else to make life complete. But what happens when the honeymoon is over? Dr. Stacey Oliker, a scientist in Wisconsin, did a study to answer that question.

Oliker wrote a book about her findings. She called it *Best Friends and Marriage.* In it she says, "Couples may find themselves in trouble if they focus solely on each other and ignore their social network. Without time apart, they may lose their sense of self and become too dependent on each other."

The study showed that strong marriages also depend on other relationships. In these marriages, both spouses have friends and family they care about besides their spouse.

Who rated happiest in the study? Dr. Oliker says, "It was the people who had a wide circle of friends, plus one or two best friends, as well as a romantic relationship."

Laurette Payne is a marriage counselor in New York City. She agrees with Oliker's study. "It doesn't matter how much you love someone. A spouse simply can't fill all of your emotional needs," Payne warns.

Choose the best answer for each question.

1. What is the main idea of the passage?
   (1) Dr. Oliker wrote a book about her study.
   (2) Most people know that falling-in-love feeling.
   (3) A marriage counselor agrees with the study.
   (4) In strong marriages, both spouses have other friends.

2. Which of the following statements is an opinion?
   (1) Stacey Oliker is a scientist in Wisconsin.
   (2) Couples should have other friends.
   (3) Dr. Oliker's book is called *Best Friends and Marriage.*
   (4) Laurette Payne is a marriage counselor.

The Fifth Time

Luis Delgado

Luis Delgado was a student at the Center for Alternative Sentencing and Employment Services (CASES) in New York City when he wrote this article.

Some of the streets of New York are bad because it's all about drugs. This used to be my life—selling drugs. I have been arrested five times for drug-related crimes, but never spent any time in the pen. It wasn't until the fifth time I was arrested that my mind got opened.

The first time I got arrested I wasn't even a drug dealer. In fact, I had never sold drugs in my life up to that point. I was on Ogden Avenue in the Bronx cutting my friend Oscar's hair. I stood over him as he sat in a chair on the sidewalk in front of a parking lot. I didn't know that Oscar was selling drugs at the time. While I was cutting his hair, an undercover cop asked me if I was selling Total Control (heroin). I told him, "No, I'm cutting my friend's hair." The cop left us, but five minutes later two blue police vans and three cop cars rushed at us from each side of the block, came to a sudden stop around us, and trapped us with no place to go. About 10 undercover cops jumped out of the vehicles. . . . They took me to the precinct and held me there 48 hours before I saw a judge. I got released, and the next day the charges were dropped. I thought it was fun getting arrested. Right after I got released I started selling drugs by taking over Oscar's business because he was still locked up.

About six months later I got arrested for the second time. I sold drugs to an undercover cop. . . . I was in jail for 27 hours. The charges were dropped the next day.

The third time I got arrested for selling drugs was about three months later. When I came before the judge, I didn't want to listen to him. He told me that if he saw me in his courtroom again, he would give me 25 years in jail, and that I wouldn't be able to see my family. When I got home that day, my mother told me to stay away from the drugs, but I didn't listen to her either. I only paid attention to my money. I didn't care how many times I got arrested.

That summer I got bagged again. It was my fourth arrest. Three days later we were released and the charges were dropped.

The fifth time I got arrested, . . . the cop found a bundle with nine bags of Total Control in it. . . . I knew for sure that I was going to do time and I was only 18 years old.

The judge asked me if I had any family present in the courtroom. My mother, my wife and my two daughters were there along with my two brothers and my sister. The judge said to me, "Luis Delgado, I'm going to make a deal with you because I feel bad putting an 18-year-old kid in jail with two daughters to support." He released me to my mother's care and sentenced me to CASES for six months. As I was leaving his courtroom, he yelled after me, "Stay out of trouble this time!"

For once in my life I listened, and today I am doing good at CASES. I am studying and building my skills so that one day I can pass the GED test and much more. I am doing a lot of art work and computer stuff. I spend more time with my family playing with my daughters and my brothers. This is the way I want my life to go.

Peace to all my people—Black, White, and Puerto Rican. Please do the right thing. Stay away from trouble or else you pay! It took me five times to wake up, but some of you may not be so lucky.

Choose the best answer for each question.

3. What caused Luis Delgado to take over Oscar's business?
   (1) Luis was charged with selling drugs.
   (2) Luis needed money.
   (3) Oscar was put in jail.
   (4) Luis cut Oscar's hair.

4. You can infer that CASES is
   (1) a prison in New York
   (2) a training program for people on probation
   (3) a place where convicts go who have children
   (4) a rehab program for heroin addicts

5. From the fourth paragraph, you can infer that Delgado sold drugs because
   (1) he was mad at his mother
   (2) the judge went easy on him
   (3) he didn't want to see his family
   (4) he wanted to make money

6. What is the theme of "The Fifth Time"?
   (1) It can be fun and easy to sell drugs.
   (2) If you get away from drugs, your life can be better.
   (3) You can make a lot of money selling drugs.
   (4) Friends can get you into trouble.

Home Is Where the Job Is

Each year, more and more people are doing their jobs from their own homes. In fact, more than 7.5 million people work at home now. Some of them work for companies, doing most of their work from home and going to the office once a week. They may have a computer at home that can access their company's computer system. Salespeople may be on the road so much that they don't have a real office at their company. Other people run their own businesses from home. These businesses include everything from auto repair to making yo-yos. Home-based businesses pump millions of dollars into the U.S. economy each year.

Working at home has many advantages. It gives people a flexible schedule. It saves them money because they don't have to pay as much for transportation, lunches, and business clothes. It also allows workers to more easily juggle child care with their jobs. As the following graph shows, more people of child-rearing age (ages 35–44) work at home than any other age group.

A good example is Mary Shaffer. She runs a beauty parlor in her house. Before she opened her business, she worked as a secretary. "I spend more time with my kids now," she says. "I'm here when they come home from school." She has raised three children while building her home-based business.

The graph below shows the number of U.S. workers in various age groups who worked at home in 1991.

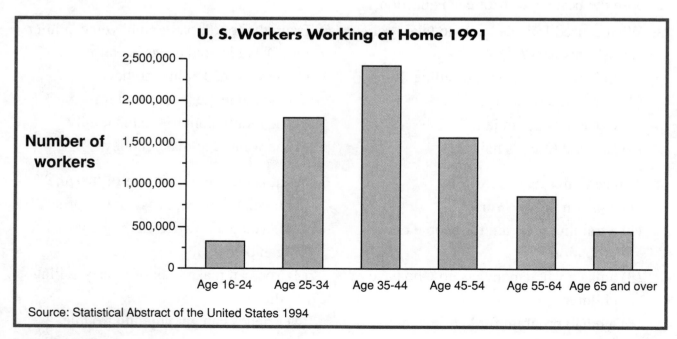

Source: Statistical Abstract of the United States 1994

Choose the best answer for each question.

7. The main idea of the second paragraph is that
   (1) people 35 to 44 are most likely to work at home
   (2) transportation can be expensive
   (3) working at home has many advantages
   (4) home-based workers have flexible schedules

8. Mary Shaffer spends more time with her children now because
   (1) she works at home
   (2) she runs a beauty parlor
   (3) there are three of them
   (4) her business is so successful

9. The passage contrasts people who work in business offices with
   (1) people who don't have jobs
   (2) people who work at home
   (3) salespeople
   (4) secretaries

10. Look at the bar for the 16–24 age group on the graph. Which other age group has almost the same number of people working at home?
    (1) age 25–34
    (2) age 35–44
    (3) age 55–64
    (4) age 65 and over

Write About It

On a separate piece of paper, write about the topic below. Then use the Revising Checklist to revise your draft.

Topic Do you think it's harder for minorities and women to find jobs than it is for other U.S. workers? Why or why not? Write one or more paragraphs to explain your opinion.

Revising Checklist

Revise your draft. Check that your draft
_____ clearly states your opinion
_____ includes reasons to support your opinion
_____ includes details or examples to explain your reasons

Skills Preview Answers

Reading Skills Preview

1. (4)		**6.** (2)	
2. (2)		**7.** (3)	
3. (3)		**8.** (1)	
4. (2)		**9.** (2)	
5. (4)		**10.** (4)	

Write About It

Make changes to your first draft to improve your writing. Then recopy your draft and share it with your instructor.

Skills Chart

The questions in the Skills Preview assess familiarity with the following skills:

Question	Skill
1	identify the main idea and details
2	identify facts and opinions
3	understand cause and effect
4	make inferences
5	make inferences
6	identify theme
7	identify the main idea and details
8	understand cause and effect
9	compare and contrast
10	compare and contrast

Unit 1 Success at Work

Success at work can mean many different things. It can mean performing your job duties well. It can mean living up to your employer's expectations. Successful workers are often team players. They respect their co-workers and are respected in return. Successful workers also take pride in their work, getting satisfaction from doing a job well. In Unit 1, you will read about people in a variety of jobs and evaluate how successful you think they are.

Before you begin Unit 1, think about how you define success at work. What would you add to or change in the description above?

▶ Be an Active Reader

As you read the selections in this unit
- Put a question mark (?) by things you do not understand.
- Underline words you do not know. Try to use context clues to figure them out.

After you read each selection in this unit
- Reread sections you marked with a question mark (?). If they still do not make sense, discuss them with a partner or your instructor.
- Look at words you underlined. Discuss any words you still don't understand with a partner or your instructor, or look them up in a dictionary.

Lesson 1

LEARNING GOALS

Strategy: Empathize with others
Reading: Read a personal account
Skill: Understand cause and effect
Writing: Explain how to do something
Life Skill: Read a paycheck stub

Before You Read

The reading in this lesson is a **personal account** about something that happened to the author. The author was a student when she wrote this account. It describes what happened when she and her husband bought a delicatessen, a store that sells cold cuts, sandwiches, and salads for takeout.

Before you read "The Deli," use the activity below to **empathize with,** or be sensitive to, the feelings of people in the story. Learning to empathize will help you better understand the characters in the stories you read. To practice, read each situation and write how you think the person feels.

1. George was alone in the new house when he heard a noise in the night. _____

   _____

2. Tomás was unfairly accused of stealing at his new job. _____

   _____

3. Elisha cheered as her daughter scored the winning basket. _____

   _____

4. Kate hurried to finish the job before closing time. _____

   _____

Preview the Reading

Before you read "The Deli," preview it. Look at the pictures. What do you think "The Deli" will be about? Do you think the woman enjoys running the business?

▶ **Use the Strategy**
As you read, try to empathize with the people in Carmen's story.
How do you think they each feel about the deli?

The Deli

Carmen Machin

My husband and I were about a year into wedded bliss, when we were made an offer we couldn't refuse. There was a delicatessen whose owner was anxious to sell. He was moving to another state. We could have the store at payments we could afford. We accepted. There was an apartment behind and connected to it which was included in the deal. We had no idea what the neighborhood was like, but with youthful energy and optimism, we moved in.

The first week was tragic. The days passed and the end of the month approached. We realized that if things continued as they were, we would not only be unable to make the payments, but would probably have to close the doors. In the midst of this anxiety was the surly attitude of the customers.

Check-in ▶ How do you think the Machins felt about their new opportunity? How would you feel?

One lady in particular seemed to enjoy my discomfort and attempts at self-control. On each of her trips into the establishment, she accused us of underweighing the cold cuts and salads or of miscounting her change. For weeks I remained courteous and patient before her onslaught. I did not want to alienate the very few customers that we had.

Then suddenly, we began to see new faces. Our business started a definite upward swing. Even our first customers seemed more pleasant. All, that is, except HER. The day came when I felt I could no longer tolerate her attacks. Still smiling, I suggested that since we did not seem to be able to satisfy her, it might be a good idea if she went elsewhere. She burst out laughing. In her thick Irish brogue[1] she proclaimed to the other customers who were there at the time, that at last she had made me show some "back-bone." Then she turned to me and said: "I wondered how long you'd be taking it." She went on to marvel at the bravery or innocence of two "spics" moving into an Irish neighborhood. I stood there in complete awe. The other customers assured me that they had, at first, abandoned the store when they heard that "spics were buying," but that, thanks to Madeline Hannon, for that was our tormentor's name, they had, one by one, come back.

---

1. brogue: strong accent, especially Irish.

Check-in ▶

Think about how Madeline Hannon felt during this confrontation with Carmen. How did Carmen feel? Can you empathize with each of them?

New York is a great big city. Most folks call it unfriendly, and yet, I never found it so. This area, from 96th Street to 100 Street, between Amsterdam and Columbus avenues, was absolutely small townish. Everyone knew everybody else and most were related in some way. Outsiders who moved in had to prove themselves worthy of acceptance or remain forever strangers. We were fortunate. Even the local gang, called the "Dukes," on whose turf our place was located, accepted us wholeheartedly.

The "Dukes," unknown to us, had terrorized all the shopkeepers in the area. In order to be able to stay in business without being harassed by vandalism, shoplifting, out and out robberies, and, in certain cases, beatings, the Dukes were paid whatever they felt the traffic would bear. In their opinion, we were to be no exception.

One day three of the young men swaggered into the store. At the time, my husband was in the cellar arranging a shipment of merchandise that had just arrived. Expecting him momentarily, I was preparing a sandwich which was to be my lunch. As I glanced up, I saw one of them quickly grab some Hostess Cupcakes and put them in his pocket. Another leaned against the fruit bin which was immediately minus an apple.

Such was my naiveté[2] that I firmly believed the only reason anyone stole food was hunger. My heart broke and at the same time opened and embraced them in the mother syndrome. They asked to speak to my husband. "He's not here at the moment. If you don't mind waiting, he should be back in a jiffy." They nodded.

Check-in ▶

What do the words "my heart broke" tell you? Do you think Carmen empathized with the three young men? How did she feel toward them?

As they started to turn to walk around the customer area, I proceeded to introduce myself and, at the same time, commenced making three more sandwiches. While I made

---

2. naiveté: innocence, trust.

small talk (actually, it was a monologue[3]) they stood silent, looking fiercely, albeit[4] hungrily, at the masterpieces I was concocting: Italian rolls, piled high with juicy roast pork and, on top, my husband's wonderful homemade cole slaw. I placed them on paper plates along with pickles and plenty of potato chips. Then I said, "Come on, you'll have to eat in the kitchen, because we're not licensed to serve in the store. Do you want milk or soda?"

"Don't you know who we are?"

"I've seen you around, but I don't know your names," I replied. They looked at me in disbelief. Shrugging their shoulders, they marched as one into the kitchen, which was the first room behind the store.

They ate to their hearts' content. Before they left, they emptied their pockets, depositing each stolen article in its appointed place. No apologies were given, none were expected. But from that day on, we were protected, and the only payment we ever made was that which we also received: friendship, trust, and acceptance.

---

3. monologue: a long speech made by one person.
4. albeit: although.

▶ **Final Check-in**

How did Carmen feel about the Dukes? How do you think the Dukes felt after Carmen gave them sandwiches?

After You Read

A. Comprehension Check

1. In the first few weeks, Machin's Deli
   (1) lost money
   (2) got new customers
   (3) became well-known
   (4) angered the gangs

2. Madeline Hannon thinks an important character trait is
   (1) empathy
   (2) bravery
   (3) patience
   (4) self-control

3. Why do the Dukes want to speak to Carmen's husband?
   (1) to order sandwiches
   (2) to apply for jobs
   (3) to warn him about other gangs
   (4) to demand protection payment

4. Why do the customers and the Dukes come to accept the Machins?
   (1) The Machins sell good sandwiches.
   (2) Carmen stood up to Madeline Hannon.
   (3) The Machins are Hispanic.
   (4) The Machins treat them with respect.

B. Revisit the Reading Strategy
Put yourself in Carmen's place. Do you think her optimism and naiveté, or innocence, helped her empathize with other people's feelings? Think about how she felt when she saw the Dukes stealing food. What other qualities might help one person empathize with another? Discuss these questions.

C. Think beyond the Reading
Carmen treated the Dukes with courtesy, and they responded with friendship, trust, and acceptance. Have you ever been suspicious of someone and then been pleasantly surprised? Have you ever thought someone was nicer than they turned out to be? Discuss these questions with a partner.

Think About It: Understand Cause and Effect

In a **cause-and-effect** relationship, one event or condition makes another one happen. The **cause** is the reason why something happens. The **effect** is the result, or outcome, of the cause.

A. Look at Cause and Effect

The effect is often mentioned first even though it happens last. Sometimes the word *because* signals a cause-and-effect relationship:

The Machins bought the deli *because* the owner made an offer they couldn't refuse.

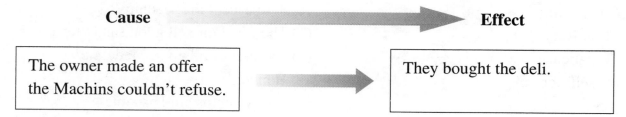

Cause → **Effect**

| The owner made an offer the Machins couldn't refuse. | → | They bought the deli. |

The word *because* won't always be there to show a cause-and-effect relationship. More often, you have to infer the relationship. Here's an example from "The Deli":

▶ There was a delicatessen whose owner was anxious to sell. He was moving to another state.

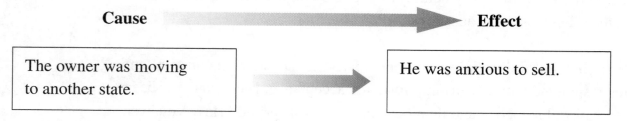

Cause → **Effect**

| The owner was moving to another state. | → | He was anxious to sell. |

B. Practice
Find the cause and the effect in the following excerpts, and fill in the boxes in your own words.

1. ▶ For weeks I remained courteous and patient before her onslaught. I did not want to alienate the very few customers that we had.

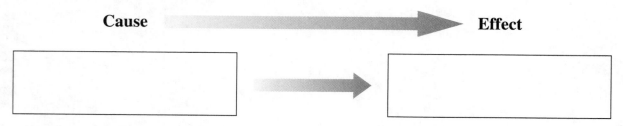

Cause → **Effect**

2. ▶ The day came when I felt I could no longer tolerate [Madeline's] attacks. Still smiling, I suggested that . . . it might be a good idea if she went elsewhere.

Cause ➡ **Effect**

3. ▶ I firmly believed the only reason anyone stole food was hunger. My heart broke and at the same time opened and embraced them in the mother syndrome.

Cause ➡ **Effect**

Find two cause-and-effect relationships in this passage.

4. ▶ The other customers assured me that they had, at first, abandoned the store when they heard that "spics were buying," but that, thanks to Madeline Hannon . . . they had . . . come back.

Cause ➡ **Effect**

▶ **Talk About It**
In a small group, **summarize** "The Deli." To summarize, you retell, in a few sentences, the most important information. Tell about
- buying the store   • the Dukes   • Madeline Hannon
- the lesson that the Machins learned

Each person in your group can summarize a different part. Be sure that together the group summarizes the whole reading selection.

Write About It: Explain How to Do Something

In every job, you need to know how to do certain tasks. In "The Deli," the author explains how she prepared sandwiches for the Dukes. In this activity, you will explain in writing how to do something.

A. **Prewriting** Think of something you know how to do well. For example, you might know how to build a bookcase, paint a room, or make a special recipe. Break the task into steps and number each step. In this example, the steps for using a computer to write something are given.

   Using a Computer to Write

   1. Turn on the monitor and the computer.

   2. Open the word processing program.

   3. Open a new file.

   4. Type a draft.

   5. Revise and edit your draft.

   6. Print a copy of your writing.

   7. Save the file containing your work.

   8. Close the file and the word processing program. Turn off the monitor and the computer.

   On separate paper, make your own list. Write the name of the task you are going to explain. Then list and number all the steps involved. List as many steps as needed.

B. **Writing** Using the numbered steps from your list, write an explanation of how to do the task. Start with a topic sentence that states the task. Then write the steps that explain how to do the task. Make sure to include enough detail so your explanation is clear.

▶ **Save your draft.** At the end of this unit, you will choose one of your drafts to work with further.

Life Skill: Read a Paycheck Stub

When their business improved, the Machins could have hired a helper. This worker would receive a weekly paycheck with a stub attached. A paycheck stub contains a summary of the worker's pay for the current pay period: hours worked, wages earned, taxes, and other deductions. The worker could cash or deposit the check at the bank, keeping the stub for her records.

Practice The paycheck stub below shows one week's earnings for Louise Twofeathers at Machin's Deli. Read it, and answer the questions that follow.

Machin's Deli	STATEMENT OF EARNINGS		WEEK ENDING	April 7

Name	Louise Twofeathers				Soc. Sec. No.	000-00-0000
PAYMENT DESCRIPTION	HOURLY RATE	NUMBER OF HOURS		GROSS THIS PERIOD		YEAR-TO-DATE
Hours Worked	$7.00	32		$224.00		$3,640.00
Sick Hours	$7.00	8		$ 56.00		$ 168.00
Vacation Hours	$7.00	0		$ 00.00		$ 112.00
TOTAL		40		$280.00		$3,920.00

TAXES	CURRENT AMOUNT/YEAR-TO-DATE		OTHER DEDUCTIONS	CURRENT AMOUNT/YEAR-TO-DATE	
Federal	$42.00	$588.00	Health Insurance	$15.00	$210.00
State	$ 7.27	$101.78	Credit Union	$10.00	$140.00
City	$ 3.94	$ 55.16			
Social Security Tax	$17.36	$243.04			
Medicare Tax	$ 4.06	$ 56.84			
TOTAL	$74.63	$1,044.82	TOTAL	$25.00	$350.00

CHECK SUMMARY	CHECK DATE	CURRENT GROSS	CURRENT TAXES & DEDUCTIONS	CURRENT NET	YEAR-TO-DATE NET
	APRIL 14	$280.00	$99.63	$180.37	$2,525.18

1. How many hours did Louise work this week? _____

2. How much was withheld from Louise's check for federal taxes this week? _____

3. How much were Louise's deductions, other than taxes? _____

4. Did Louise have any sick time this week? If so, how much? _____

5. How much did Louise take home after taxes and deductions? _____

Lesson 2

LEARNING GOALS

Strategy: Use your prior experience
Reading: Read job performance evaluations
Skill: Identify facts and opinions
Writing: Write a performance evaluation
Life Skill: Fill in a vacation request form

Before You Read

In "Evaluation Time" you will read about three employees of a company. The reading selection also includes these employees' job performance evaluations. The evaluations were written by their supervisors. You can use your **prior experience**—your own past experiences, observations, and reading—to help you understand what you read. Have you ever been evaluated by someone for a job you have done? What skills, actions, or attitudes do you think employers evaluate? On the lines below, list some things a supervisor might consider when evaluating a worker.

_____

_____

_____

Preview the Reading

Preview "Evaluation Time" by looking at how the performance evaluation forms are organized. Notice that there is a place on each form for the supervisor's comments.

▶ **Use the Strategy**
As you read, use your prior experience to judge each employee's job performance. Who was rated highly? Who was given a warning?

Evaluation Time

Bluebell Foods, Inc., has a chain of 15 pastry shops throughout the city. It employs many people. All employees are regularly evaluated by their immediate supervisors. Alice Ling is having her annual evaluation. Felipe Gonzalez and Jill Blanchard are having their first evaluation since being hired six months ago.

Alice Ling is the company receptionist at corporate headquarters. Her main duties are answering the phone, greeting people, and handling the mail. Since she is the first person many customers and vendors see, she must be well-groomed. Alice never finished high school. She was hired soon after Bluebell opened and has worked for the company for 30 years.

Felipe Gonzalez is a warehouse worker in his early thirties. He completed preparatory school—similar to high school in the U.S., but more advanced—in his home country, Mexico. He transports and stacks pastry mixes. The mixes come in 100-pound sacks, which are stored in boxes on flats. Felipe stacks the flats with a forklift, making sure the different mixes are stacked in their proper place in the warehouse. He has to work fast but without damaging anything. Safety and cleanliness are top priorities in his job.

Jill Blanchard, a high school junior, is a part-time sales clerk at the shop in Mt. Pleasant. She must operate the cash register, make change, and respond to customers' requests. She has to be familiar with sales promotions. To increase sales, she is supposed to suggest additional items to customers. The company wants the clerks to be helpful and pleasant to customers, but visits from friends are discouraged. Appearance and hygiene are important.

Check-in ▶ Which of the three employees do you think would get the highest rating? Why do you think so?

Performance evaluations for these three employees are shown below.
E stands for Excellent, **S** for Satisfactory, **N** for Needs Improvement,
and **U** for Unsatisfactory.

Annual Performance Review

Employee name: Alice Ling
Position: Receptionist
Supervisor: Willard Mendey

	E	S	N	U
Knows how to do the job			x	
Is dependable		x		
Is punctual		x		
Works hard		x		
Is polite to customers and/or co-workers		x		
Dresses appropriately		x		
Operates equipment competently			x	

Comments: Alice does a wonderful job in many ways. She's good with people and always willing to stay late when we need her. Her only problem is that she's having a hard time learning the new phone system. I'm going to arrange for additional training for her.

Initial Performance Evaluation

Employee name: Felipe Gonzalez
Position: Warehouse Transporter
Supervisor: Jon Dory

	E	S	N	U
Knows how to do the job		x		
Is dependable		x		
Is punctual		x		
Works hard	x			
Is polite to customers and/or co-workers			x	
Dresses appropriately		x		
Operates equipment competently				x

Comments: Felipe works hard and does a good job. I've seen him lift two 100-pound sacks at once. He keeps the warehouse well-organized. But he is short-tempered with his co-workers. I've told him to "count to 10" and give himself a cooling off period before dealing with a situation that makes him angry. I have also told him that sometimes he drives the forklift too fast. Once he ran into a flat and hit a box, puncturing it and spilling its contents. So I'm going to write him up each time I see him speeding.

Initial Performance Evaluation

Employee name: Jill Blanchard
Position: Sales Clerk
Supervisor: Lisa Kinski

	E	S	N	U
Knows how to do the job			x	
Is dependable		x		
Is punctual			x	
Works hard		x		
Is polite to customers and/or co-workers	x			
Dresses appropriately		x		
Operates equipment competently			x	

Comments: Jill is very good with customers, but she has made several mistakes on the cash register. I've told her to slow down when ringing up sales to be more accurate. I'm going to suggest a business math course. I've had to warn Jill twice about coming in late, and once I had to ask her friends to leave the store. I'm afraid Jill's more interested in her social life than in her job. I reminded her that after a third warning, she may be fired.

▶ **Final Check-in**

Have you ever had a performance evaluation? In what ways was it similar to these? How was it different?

After You Read

A. Comprehension Check

1. Alice Ling went to work for Bluebell Foods
   (1) after high school graduation
   (2) six months ago
   (3) 30 years ago
   (4) when Bluebell had 15 stores

2. Felipe Gonzalez
   (1) is from Spain
   (2) works in a pastry shop
   (3) operates a forklift
   (4) is not very strong

3. Jill Blanchard
   (1) is very punctual
   (2) is good at math
   (3) doesn't have many friends
   (4) is good with customers

4. Bluebell Foods
   (1) has a new phone system
   (2) sells mainly meat and fish
   (3) has shops throughout the state
   (4) employs mostly women

5. Which employee do you think is in danger of getting fired? Why? _____

   _____

B. Revisit the Reading Strategy
Read the statements below. Using your prior experience, state whether you agree or disagree with each one and why.

1. A performance evaluation is the best way to judge an employee's job skills. _____

   _____

2. An employer has no business telling workers what to wear. _____

   _____

3. You can take pride in any job. _____

   _____

C. Think beyond the Reading
Think about a performance evaluation you have had. Did you think it was fair? How would you rate yourself as an employee? Make a form like the ones on page 26 and mark the areas in which you think your work is Excellent, is Satisfactory, Needs Improvement, or is Unsatisfactory. Compare charts with a partner. Discuss the qualities of a good employee.

Think About It: Identify Facts and Opinions

A **fact** is a statement that can be shown to be true. An **opinion** is a statement of belief, a guess, or a prediction. For example, you might say, "Joe makes pies at the Bluebell Pastry Shop." That's a fact. It can be shown to be true. But if you say, "Joe makes the best pies in town," that's an opinion. It cannot be shown to be true.

The first page of "Evaluation Time" is factual. It consists mainly of job descriptions. But the evaluations themselves contain both facts and opinions. Notice how this supervisor gave two opinions before stating one fact:

▶ Alice does a wonderful job in many ways. She's good with people and always willing to stay late when we need her.

The only fact here is that Alice is always willing to stay late. The statements that she does a wonderful job and is good with people are opinions.

A. Look at Facts and Opinions

To decide whether a statement is a fact or an opinion, ask yourself whether it can be shown to be true. You'll find opinions you agree with and opinions you disagree with, but opinions can't be shown to be true.

In this example from the performance evaluations, which statements are facts? Which are opinions?

▶ Felipe works hard and does a good job. I've seen him lift two 100-pound sacks at once.

Fact: Felipe can lift two 100-pound sacks at once.

Opinions: Felipe works hard and does a good job.

B. Practice Read each statement and write **F** for Fact or **O** for Opinion next to each one.

_____ **1.** Bluebell Foods, Inc., has a chain of 15 pastry shops.

_____ **2.** Bluebell Foods employs good workers.

_____ **3.** Alice Ling has worked for Bluebell too long.

_____ **4.** Alice Ling did not graduate from high school.

_____ **5.** Alice might not be able to learn the new phone system.

_____ **6.** Alice has worked for Bluebell Foods for 30 years.

_____ **7.** Felipe Gonzalez has worked for Bluebell Foods for six months.

_____ **8.** Felipe completed preparatory school in his home country, Mexico.

_____ **9.** Once Felipe hit a flat and punctured a box.

_____ **10.** Felipe has to learn to control his temper.

_____ **11.** Jill Blanchard is having her first job evaluation.

_____ **12.** Jill is good with the customers.

_____ **13.** She has made several mistakes on the cash register.

_____ **14.** Jill has been warned twice about coming in late.

_____ **15.** She seems more interested in her social life than her job.

▶ **Talk About It**

With a partner, role-play one of the performance evaluations in the reading. For example, one partner can play Jill Blanchard, the sales clerk, while the other plays the role of her supervisor, Lisa Kinski. Sit down and discuss Jill's job performance. As her supervisor, you may add qualities, both good and bad, to the evaluation. Make sure you tell Jill what she's doing right. When you discuss what needs improvement, give her specific suggestions. When you're finished, switch roles. You can also role-play evaluation meetings between Alice Ling and Felipe Gonzalez and their supervisors.

▶ **Discuss** Which role did you enjoy more, the employee or the supervisor? Why?

Write About It: Write a Performance Evaluation

In "Evaluation Time," you read what three supervisors had to say about their employees' job performance. Supervisors are also evaluated by their supervisors. In this activity, you will write an evaluation of a supervisor.

A. Prewriting Start by thinking about a supervisor you have had, or imagine the supervisors at Bluebell Foods. Think about the qualities, actions, or abilities of a good supervisor. For example, you might think supervisors should understand the demands of each job they supervise. You might also think it is important that supervisors treat everyone fairly and address people politely. Below is a sample evaluation form based on the ideas above. Think of other qualities or abilities you would add.

Annual Performance Review

Employee Name: _____   Position: _Supervisor_____

Supervisor: _____

	E	S	N	U
Plans and organizes to meet objectives				
Delegates responsibility and authority				
Establishes reasonable performance goals				
Monitors and gives follow-up effectively				
Willingly makes timely decisions				
Treats all employees fairly and politely				
Understands demands of each job being supervised				

Comments: _____

B. Writing Draw your chart on separate paper. Add the qualities, actions, and abilities that you think supervisors should have. Then rate a real or imagined supervisor by completing the ratings. Look back at the performance evaluations in this lesson as a model. In the comment section, point out a good quality and a special problem the supervisor has. Tell at least one way the supervisor can improve in the problem area.

▶ **Save your draft.** At the end of this unit, you will choose one of your drafts to work with further.

Life Skill: Fill In a Vacation Request Form

At Bluebell Foods and most other companies, employees fill in vacation request forms. They choose their vacation time weeks—sometimes months—in advance. Coordinating the dates early is important so that no department is understaffed, even during the most popular vacation times.

Practice Read the calendar and vacation request form below, and answer the questions that follow.

JUNE							JULY							AUGUST						
S	M	T	W	T	F	S	S	M	T	W	T	F	S	S	M	T	W	T	F	S
	1	2	3	4	5	6				1	2	3	4							1
7	8	9	10	11	12	13	5	6	7	8	9	10	11	2	3	4	5	6	7	8
14	15	16	17	18	19	20	12	13	14	15	16	17	18	9	10	11	12	13	14	15
21	22	23	24	25	26	27	19	20	21	22	23	24	25	16	17	18	19	20	21	22
28	29	30					26	27	28	29	30	31		23	24	25	26	27	28	29
														30	31					

Name: _Alice Ling_   Soc. Sec. # _000-00-0000_
Dept.: _Admin._   Job Title: _Receptionist_

List your first choice of vacation days and dates.
Then list your second and third choices in case of schedule conflicts.

First choice: _____ August 3-August 14 _____
Second choice: _____ June 1-June 12 _____
Third choice: _____ July 13-July 24 _____
How many workdays will you be gone? ___10_____

1. How many workdays is Alice taking off? _____

2. If she gets her first choice, how many days in a row will Alice be on vacation? (Note: Include weekends.) _____

3. Choose your own summer vacation days. Assume you get two weeks, or 10 working days, and that you must take off consecutive weeks. Under-line your first choice on the calendar with a double line. Underline your second choice with a single line. Form a group of four or five people. Imagine you all work in the same department. Compare schedules to see if any vacations overlap. If they do, negotiate and adjust the schedules until each person has a satisfactory vacation schedule.

Lesson 3

LEARNING GOALS

Strategy: Skim reading material
Reading: Read an article
Skill: Identify the main idea and details
Writing: Write a business letter
Life Skill: Read a bar graph

Before You Read

The article in this lesson describes things you can do to be more successful at work. Think about people you know who are successful at their jobs. What are some of the qualities that these people share? Check the qualities below that you think are important for success in your work. Add one or two ideas of your own.

_____ dependability   _____ strength   _____ good people skills

_____ honesty   _____ carefulness   _____

_____ punctuality   _____ neatness   _____

Preview the Reading

Preview "How to Be Successful at Work" by **skimming** the title and all the headings. Look at the pictures, lists, and graph. What do you think the article will tell you? Think about the headings. What topics do you think the article will discuss?

▶ **Use the Strategy**
You skimmed all the headings and the lists in the article to get a general idea of what the article is about. Now, guided by what you learned from skimming, read to find specific information.

How to Be Successful at Work

Wherever your job is—in a factory, at a store, in an office, at home—there are certain things you need to know in order to be successful at work. Sometimes you learn those things from your own work experiences—both good and bad. You can also learn from reading about other people's experiences. This article tells about several people and their experiences at work. It will give you advice about being successful at your job.

Choose the Right Job for You

"I work only four hours a day," Fay sighed. "But it is very tiring." Fay, age 48, is a dishwasher in a small restaurant. "You have to be strong to do this job," she continued. "You are always on your feet and don't get many breaks." As you can see, Fay must be able to meet the tough physical demands of her job in order to do it well.

Jobs can be mentally demanding as well. You need to know your mental strengths and weaknesses and choose a job that takes them into account. For example, someone who is not good with numbers probably will not succeed as a bookkeeper. A person who gets bored easily probably will not excel at a job that involves repetitive tasks like copying and collating.

It is also important to identify your interests and what matters to you. Hanan, a very outgoing woman, is a ski instructor. "I meet a lot of people," she beamed. "And I get to be outdoors all day. It is a beautiful job." Being with people is important to Hanan. Doing work she likes helps her succeed at her job.

Another important aspect of choosing a job is compensation. Ideally, you can find a job with salary and benefits that fit your needs. Also consider whether you can adjust your lifestyle to fit your work schedule. Schedule, salary, and benefits that don't fit your needs can create stress. If you are under stress, you are less likely to perform well on the job or to enjoy it.

Know What the Boss Expects

What does your employer expect of you? Here are some basic commonsense expectations of any job:

- Learn your job fairly quickly.
- Perform your duties in a reasonable amount of time.
- Always be on time for work.
- Don't take long breaks.

When you skim, lists jump out at you. What information did you get quickly from the list above?

◀ Check-in

In any job it's important to be honest, dependable, and willing to work. Successful workers acquire other qualities as well, depending on the job. Bill works in his company's stockroom. "I learned to be patient, follow orders, and pay close attention."

Employers expect their employees to present a good image of the company. Employees should be neat and clean, including those like Bill who do not work directly with customers. Those who have contact with customers and clients must be especially well groomed. This is also true of employees who work in the front office of a company.

Safety is an issue on many jobs. If your job involves lifting, working with machines, or handling hazardous materials, make a point of learning the best way to do these things. Many employers provide specific training for workers who work around machinery or hazardous materials.

Some Tips on Getting Along with People

Sabrina is a server in a coffee shop. "I have learned how to deal with people on my job," she explained. "My communication with co-workers and customers has improved since I've been here."

Sabrina's behavior reflects this attitude. She is friendly and polite to customers. She has also learned how to handle difficult situations. "Sometimes people come into the shop in a bad mood," Sabrina went on. "They want to argue with other customers. I serve them fast and send them on their way."

Another way to get along well with people at work is to follow these two pieces of advice: Don't discuss personal problems on the job, and don't gossip. You don't want to get a reputation as a complainer or troublemaker. Your boss will appreciate your restraint, and so will your co-workers.

Reach beyond Your Job Description

Raymond is a cook in a busy restaurant. "Even when the restaurant is not busy, there is always something to do," he said. "Use your free time to help or learn. If you don't see anything to do, ask if a fellow worker needs help."

Marian had the same idea. She is a bookkeeper in an accounting firm. The government frequently passes new laws or changes guidelines for accounting. There is always something new to learn. "Use your spare time to learn more," she urged.

Some Final Notes

The job market is always changing. A worker today must be motivated and adapt to those changes. Don't be afraid to ask your supervisor and co-workers questions, and don't be discouraged if you slip up. Just be sure you learn from any mistakes. Above all, don't be afraid to come up with new ideas to solve a problem. This shows you have imagination and are a self-starter.[1]

Choosing a Job with Success in Mind

Many factors should be considered when planning a new career. Among the most important are

- the skills necessary to do the job
- how much money the job pays
- the number of jobs available or likely to be available in the field

The graph below shows what occupations are likely to grow the fastest from 1992 to 2005. Notice that the number of jobs for home health aides is expected to increase by almost 140 percent in that time. An increase in jobs in a field is not the only factor to consider when choosing a career. You need to take into account your needs, skills, interests, and personality, too.

---

1. self-starter: a worker who takes initiative, who will start an action.

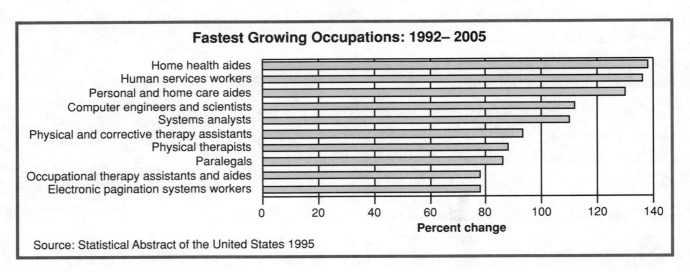

Fastest Growing Occupations: 1992– 2005

Source: Statistical Abstract of the United States 1995

Final Check-in

When you skimmed the article, did the headings tell you what to expect in each section? Did the article meet your expectations? Why or why not?

After You Read

A. Comprehension Check

1. The article discusses
   - (1) negotiating for a raise
   - (2) reasons for downturns in the economy
   - (3) what classes to take in school
   - (4) choosing the right job

2. To get along with co-workers, one must
   - (1) communicate well with them
   - (2) like them
   - (3) gossip with them
   - (4) discuss personal problems with them

3. Bosses expect workers to
   - (1) know everything
   - (2) have uniforms
   - (3) waste time
   - (4) be willing to learn

4. According to the graph, the second-fastest-growing occupation is
   - (1) human services workers
   - (2) personal and home care aides
   - (3) physical therapists
   - (4) systems analysts

B. Revisit the Reading Strategy After reading an article, you may want to locate a specific piece of information in it. You can find it by skimming the article again. Skim the article and the graph to answer the questions.

1. What was the list on page 34 about? _____

   _____

2. To get along with people at work, what should you avoid doing? _____

   _____

3. Skim the graph again. Which of the fastest growing jobs would you be most interested in? _____

C. Think beyond the Reading How might you use the ideas in this article to help you succeed on the job? With a partner, discuss things you need to do to be successful at work.

Think About It: Identify the Main Idea and Details

The **main idea** is the central thought or meaning of a passage—what the passage is all about. **Details** provide specific facts, examples, or reasons that support or explain the main idea. In articles like "How to Be Successful at Work," there is a general main idea for the whole article and a specific main idea for each section. The main idea of the whole article can be stated as "This article gives advice about how to be successful at work." The main idea for the section "Some Tips on Getting Along with People" can be stated as "It is important to get along well with customers and your co-workers."

Within each section, each paragraph will also have a main idea. The main idea of the paragraph below is underlined.

> ▶ Wherever your job is—in a factory, at a store, in an office, at home—<u>there are certain things you need to know in order to be successful at work</u>. Sometimes you learn those things from your own work experiences—both good and bad. You can also learn from reading about other people's experiences. This article tells about several people and their experiences at work. It will give you advice about being successful at your job.

The main idea is stated in the first sentence. It is supported by two details: You can learn from your own work experiences, and from the advice and experience of other people.

A. Look at Main Idea and Details

To identify the main idea, look for what the passage is about in general. Then look for information that provides details about the main idea. Find the main idea and details in the following paragraph.

> ▶ Marian had the same idea. She is a bookkeeper in an accounting firm. The government frequently passes new laws or changes guidelines for accounting. There is always something new to learn. "Use your spare time to learn more," she urged.

The main idea in the paragraph is "There is always something new to learn." The details are reasons why Marian's job requires constant learning to keep up with changes in her field.

B. Practice Read each paragraph and underline the main idea. Then check the type of detail used to support the main idea.

1. ▶ Jobs can be mentally demanding as well. You need to know your mental strengths and weaknesses and choose a job that takes them into account. For example, someone who is not good with numbers probably will not succeed as a bookkeeper. A person who gets bored easily probably will not excel at a job that involves repetitive tasks like copying and collating.

   Are the details _____ facts? _____ examples? _____ reasons?

2. ▶ Another important aspect of choosing a job is compensation. Ideally, you can find a job with salary and benefits that fit your needs. Also consider whether you can adjust your lifestyle to fit your work schedule. Schedule, salary, and benefits that don't fit your needs can create stress. If you are under stress, you are less likely to perform well on the job or to enjoy it.

   Are the details _____ facts? _____ examples? _____ reasons?

3. ▶ What does your employer expect of you? Here are some basic commonsense expectations of any job:
   • Learn your job fairly quickly.
   • Perform your duties in a reasonable amount of time.
   • Always be on time for work.
   • Don't take long breaks.

   Are the details _____ facts? _____ examples? _____ reasons?

4. ▶ "I work only four hours a day," Fay sighed. "But it is very tiring." Fay, age 48, is a dishwasher in a small restaurant. "You have to be strong to do this job," she continued. "You are always on your feet and don't get many breaks." As you can see, Fay must be able to meet the tough physical demands of her job in order to do it well.

   Are the details _____ facts? _____ examples? _____ reasons?

▶ **Talk About It**
The article gave two pieces of advice for getting along with people at work: Don't discuss personal problems, and don't gossip. In a small group, discuss some positive things people can do to get along well with others at work. List your group's ideas and then share them with the whole group.

Write About It: Write a Business Letter

A well-written letter of application is an important part of a successful job search. Your letter of application, plus a resume of your educational background and work experience, introduces you to a prospective employer. Use the form of a **business letter** to write a letter of application.

Business letters follow a particular format. Look at the sample below. It starts with the sender's address, then the date, then the receiver's name and address. Note the colon after the greeting "Dear Ms. Brown." The body of the letter should be informative and brief. Usually three paragraphs are adequate for a letter of application. The letter closes with "Sincerely" and the sender's signature and name printed or typed. If you are enclosing anything, such as a resume, type "enc." at the bottom of the page.

A. Prewriting

Think of a job you might like. Make a list of reasons why you are qualified for the job. Include your skills, background, and interests.

B. Writing

Write a letter applying for a job. Use the business letter format. Start your letter by stating the job you are applying for. Explain why you think you would do a good job for the company. Direct attention to the information in your resume. Close with a request for an interview and a thank-you.

▶ **Save your draft.** At the end of this unit, you will choose one of your drafts to work with further.

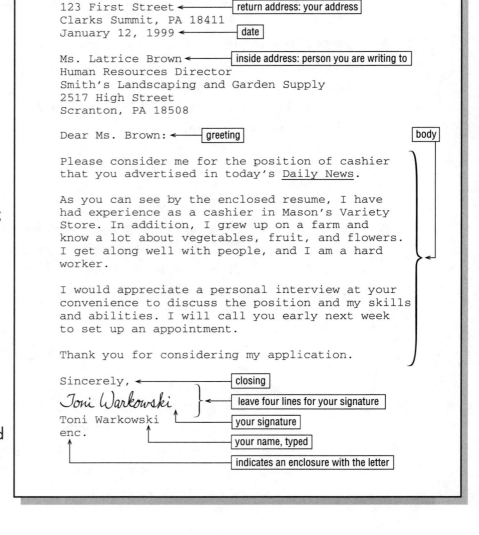

123 First Street ← return address: your address
Clarks Summit, PA 18411
January 12, 1999 ← date

Ms. Latrice Brown ← inside address: person you are writing to
Human Resources Director
Smith's Landscaping and Garden Supply
2517 High Street
Scranton, PA 18508

Dear Ms. Brown: ← greeting   body

Please consider me for the position of cashier that you advertised in today's Daily News.

As you can see by the enclosed resume, I have had experience as a cashier in Mason's Variety Store. In addition, I grew up on a farm and know a lot about vegetables, fruit, and flowers. I get along well with people, and I am a hard worker.

I would appreciate a personal interview at your convenience to discuss the position and my skills and abilities. I will call you early next week to set up an appointment.

Thank you for considering my application.

Sincerely, ← closing
Toni Warkowski } ← leave four lines for your signature
Toni Warkowski ← your signature
enc. ← your name, typed
← indicates an enclosure with the letter

Life Skill: Another Look at Reading a Bar Graph

Graphs are used in place of words to display certain kinds of information. **Bar graphs** are especially helpful in making comparisons. The bar graph on page 36 showed the occupations that are projected to grow the fastest between 1992 and 2005. The bar graph below shows the occupations projected to have the largest numbers of new jobs from 1992 to 2005. To read it, read the title and the labels at the bottom and along the side. The labels on the left show occupations with the largest potential growth and the bottom labels show the numbers of new jobs. The length of each bar represents the projected number of new jobs in that occupation between 1992 and 2005.

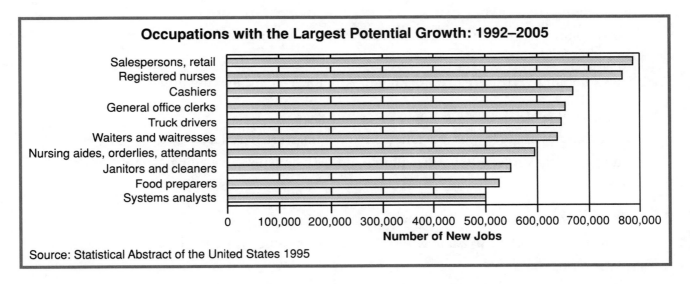

Occupations with the Largest Potential Growth: 1992–2005

Source: Statistical Abstract of the United States 1995

Practice Study the graph and answer these questions about it.

1. Which occupation is projected to have the most new jobs by the year 2005?
2. About how many new cashier jobs are projected between 1992 and 2005?
3. About how many new truck drivers will be needed?
4. About how many new systems analysts will be needed?
5. Look back at the graph on page 36. By what percentage is the systems analyst job category expected to grow during this same time period?
6. Compare the graph above with the graph on page 36. Why don't the two graphs list the same jobs in the same order?

▶ Writing Skills Mini-Lesson:
Subject-Verb Agreement with *be* and *have*

Every sentence has a **subject** (who or what the sentence is about) and a **verb** (what the subject does or is). The verb can be a single verb. In this case, the single verb is called the **main verb.** The verb may also be a **verb phrase** consisting of a main verb and other verbs, such as *is going* or *have known.* The other verbs in a verb phrase are called **helping verbs.** Both *be* and *have* can be the main verb in a sentence. *Be* and *have* can also be helping verbs. When *be* and *have* stand alone as main verbs or act as helping verbs, they must **agree** with their subjects. Follow these rules:

1. **The present tense of the verb *be* has three forms: *am, is,* and *are.***
    Used as main verbs: I **am** a sales associate. Steven **is** a nurse. We **are** a team.
    Used as helping verbs: We **are working** in Atlanta. You **are looking** great!

2. **The past tense of *be* has two forms: *was* and *were.***
    Used as main verbs: He **was** a teacher. My cousins **were** here last week.
    Used as helping verbs: He **was teaching** math. My cousins **were going** home.

3. **The present tense of *have* has two forms: *have* and *has.***
    Used as main verbs: I **have** a new job. My sister **has** a new job. We both **have** new jobs.
    Used as helping verbs: She **has worked** here for two months. They **have learned** new skills.
    Note: The past tense of *have* has only one form: *had.*

Practice Copy the paragraph, making all the verbs agree with their subjects.

> I has always believed in Marco. Marco is my boyfriend. He have a good job as a chef. He have been working at the restaurant for two years. Just a few years ago, Marco was out of work. His relatives was very worried about him, but I were not. I were sure he were going to find a good job. Now we is all happy for Marco.

Unit 1 Review

Reading Review

Learning on the Job

One way to succeed on the job is to continue learning. The world changes fast, and workers have to learn new skills to keep up.

Mastering Computer Skills

If you work in an office, you already know how important computer skills are. Mastering word processing or graphics programs can make you a more valuable employee. It may also help you get promoted.

These days, it's not just office workers who are using computers. Line workers in steel mills and press operators at printing companies must use computers, too. Salespeople use laptop computers to send sales data back to the head office. In some restaurants, servers use handheld computers to send food orders to the kitchen electronically.

Serving Your Customers

You've probably heard the saying, "The customer is always right." In our competitive world, that's more true than ever, and now "customer" is being defined more broadly.

Not only are you concerned with external customers—the people who buy your company's product or use its services—but you have to please internal customers, too. For example, suppose you work in the warehouse of a big discount store. Every salesperson wants to make sure his or her section is stocked with enough merchandise. They are your internal customers. If you work in the accounting department, every employee whose paychecks or W-2 forms pass through your hands is your customer. Mastering this attitude helps everyone in the organization become more productive.

Continuing Your Education

You can keep up-to-date through continuing education. Smart employers know that it's well worth the cost to send workers to classes to improve their current skills and learn new ones. If you want to take a class, give your boss examples of how you will be more productive as a result. Employers are usually happy to hear their employees are willing to take on more training. You benefit by learning new skills and increasing your worth on the job market.

Choose the best answer to each question.

1. According to the article, computers are used in many businesses so
   (1) you should apply for jobs that don't use computers
   (2) customers need computer skills
   (3) mastering computer programs can help you get ahead
   (4) you won't need computer skills in the future

2. Which of the following is an opinion?
   (1) Pleasing internal customers helps everyone in the organization become more productive.
   (2) Press operators at printing plants use computers.
   (3) External customers are the people who buy a company's product.
   (4) Continuing education classes can teach you new skills.

3. What is the main idea of this article?
   (1) You can't get a job without a computer.
   (2) It's important to keep learning on the job.
   (3) The customer is always right.
   (4) Classes are worth the cost.

The Writing Process

In Unit 1, you wrote three first drafts. Choose the piece that you would like to work with further. You will revise, edit, and make a final copy of the draft.

_____ your explanation of how to do something (page 22)
_____ your performance evaluation of a supervisor (page 30)
_____ your business letter applying for a job (page 40)

Find the first draft of your choice. Then turn to page 159 in this book. Follow steps 3, 4, and 5 in the Writing Process to create a final draft.

As you revise, check your draft for these specific points:

Explanation: Make sure you use details to explain each step in the task.
Performance evaluation: Be sure the comment section mentions a good quality the supervisor has and tells how the supervisor can improve.
Letter of application: Be sure you have stated the job you are applying for, mentioned your skills that apply to the job, and asked for an interview.

Unit 2 Taking a Stand

At some time in our lives, most of us will face a situation that will challenge us to stand up for what we believe in. We may witness an injustice. Someone we know and admire may be discriminated against because of race, religion, or gender. Someone may be unjustly blamed for something. How we respond to these challenges depends upon many things: the strength of our beliefs, our courage at the time, the cost of taking a stand and speaking out.

The readings in this unit are about four real people who risked their lives to stand up for their beliefs. Before you read Unit 2, think of a time when you or someone you know took a stand. Did it take courage? Did it make a difference?

▶ **Be an Active Reader**

As you read the selections in this unit
- Put a question mark (?) by things you do not understand.
- <u>Underline</u> words you do not know. Try to use context clues to figure them out.

After you read each selection in this unit
- Reread sections you marked with a question mark (?). If they still do not make sense, discuss them with a partner or your instructor.
- Look at words you <u>underlined</u>. Discuss any words you still don't understand with a partner or your instructor, or look them up in a dictionary.

Lesson 4

LEARNING GOALS

Strategy: Use your prior knowledge
Reading: Read a story
Skill: Identify theme
Writing: Write about an incident
Life Skill: Read a political cartoon

Before You Read

In "The Right Thing to Do at the Time," the author's father takes a stand against racism. The story takes place in Florida in the 1930s, during the Great Depression. Poverty was widespread in the U.S. at that time. There was also much racial prejudice, particularly in the South, against African Americans.

When you read this story, use your **prior knowledge**—knowledge you have gained from personal experience and learning—to help you understand it. Have you seen movies and television shows about the Great Depression? Have you read about the Civil Rights movement of the 1960s? Think of what you know about prejudice against African Americans before the passage of civil rights laws in the 1960s. Think of what you've heard and read about the Depression of the 1930s. On the lines below, list two things that you know about life during the Depression. Then list two things you know about treatment of African Americans during that time.

_____   _____

_____   _____

Preview the Reading

To preview "The Right Thing to Do at the Time," look at the title and the pictures. What do you think will happen in this story?

▶ **Use the Strategy**

As you read, use your background knowledge to better understand the story. Think about the conditions at that time, the difficulties African Americans faced, and how dangerous it was to defend them.

The Right Thing to Do at the Time

George Garrett

My father was a small-town southern lawyer, not a writer, but he was a truth teller. And he would tell the truth, come what may, hell or high water. And since he loved the truth and would gladly risk his life (and ours, the whole family's) for the sake of it, he would fight without stint, withholding nothing, offering no pity or quarter against what he took to be wrong—that is, against the untruth. He would go to any length he had to. And that is what this story is all about—how far one man would go to fight for the truth and against what was and is wrong.

We were living in the cow town of Kissimmee, Florida, in the early years of the Great Depression. Disney World is near there now, and it looks pretty much like everyplace else. But it was a hard, tough place then, a place where life was hard for many decent people, black and white. And it was a place where some not-so-decent people had managed to seize power and to hold power and were extremely unlikely to be dislodged from power. Among the people in power in those days were the Ku Klux Klan, not a sad little bunch of ignorant racists in bedsheets but a real clan, a native-grown kind of organized crime family.

My father and his law partner were fighting against the Klan in court and in public with the promise that they would (as they, in fact, did) represent free of charge any person at all who chose to resist the Klan and wanted a lawyer.

This exposed position led to a whole lot of trouble, believe me. And in the end it led to the demise[1] of the Klan as a power of any kind in central Florida. But the big trouble came later. This happened early on as the lines were being drawn and the fight was just getting under way.

---

1. demise: death.

Sometimes in the early evening we would go together, my mother and father and the other children, into town for an ice-cream cone: a great treat in those days. One evening we piled into our old car and drove into the center of town and parked in front of the drugstore. Went inside and sat on tall swivel chairs at the counter eating our ice-cream cones.

We were all sitting there in a row when a young policeman walked in. Try as I will, I can't remember his name anymore. Just that he was very young and that my mother, who was a teacher then, had taught him in high school. He greeted her politely at first. He seemed a little awkward and embarrassed.

"Mr. Garrett," he said to my father, "I'm afraid I'm going to have to give you a red ticket."

"Oh, really?" my father said, still licking his ice-cream cone. "What for?"

"Well, sir, your taillights don't work."

"They did when I came down here."

"Well, sir, they sure don't now."

"Let's us have a look."

So we all trooped outside and looked at the taillights. They didn't work, all right, because they were broken and there was shattered red glass all over the street right behind the back bumper.

"I wonder who would do a thing like that," my father said, giving the young cop a hard look.

Check-in

What do you think Mr. Garrett suspected when he looked at his broken tail-lights and then at the police-man? What do you suspect happened?

"Well, I wouldn't know, sir," he said. "I just work for the city and I do what I'm told. And I have to write you a ticket."

"Fine," my father said. "I understand that."

Then he surprised the cop and us too by asking if he could pay for the ticket right then and there. And the cop said yes, that was his legal right, and he said it would cost five dollars.

Now, that was considerable money in those days when grown men with some skills were earning eight or ten dollars a week. Nobody had any money in those days, nobody we knew or knew of.

Most of my father's clients, those who could pay at all, paid him in produce and fresh eggs, things like that.

My father peeled off five one-dollar bills. The cop wrote him a receipt. Then my father told my mother to drive us on home when we had finished our ice cream. He had to go somewhere right away.

He whistled loudly and waved his arm for a taxi. One came right over from the Atlantic Coastline depot directly across the way. He kissed my mother on the cheek and said he would be back just as soon as he could. Gave her the keys to our car and hopped into the cab.

None of us heard what he told the driver: "Let's go to Tallahassee."

Tallahassee was and is the state capital, a good 300 or so miles away by bad, narrow roads in those days.

Much later we learned what happened. They arrived very late. Slept in the cab. First thing in the morning he got himself a shave in the barbershop. Then went to the legislature. Where, exercising a constitutional right to speak on this kind of matter, he quickly established that the town charter for Kissimmee, Florida, was completely illegal and unconstitutional. In a technical, legal sense that town did not exist and never had. It would require a special action of the state legislature to give the town a new charter and a legal existence. Having made his point, he thanked the legislators kindly and left the capitol. Woke the snoring taxi driver and said, "Let's go back home."

It probably cost him a hundred dollars for that ride. Maybe more. He never told us, and nobody, not even my mother, ever dared ask him.

By the time he arrived home there was a delegation waiting to see him at our house: the mayor, the chief of police, the judge, pretty much the whole gang. Legislators had been on the phone all day to them, and they were deeply worried. Because, you see, everything they had ever done, in the absence of a valid town charter, including collecting taxes, had been illegal. You can imagine what that would mean if people got it in mind to be litigious[2] about things.

---

2. litigious: eager to start a lawsuit.

Everybody came into our living room. And the whole family, too, because, he said, we saw the beginning of it and deserved to see the end.

Before the mayor or any of them said a word, he explained to them exactly what he had done. And he told them that, under the state constitution, establishing a town was a very tricky legal business. He said the chances were a hundred to one that they would mess it up again. He wished them good luck, promising that if they ever bothered him or us anymore, he would go to Tallahassee again and close them down for keeps.

There was a lot of silence. Finally the mayor spoke.

"What do you want from us, Garrett?"

"Ah," said my father. "I knew it would come down to that. And I'm glad it did, because there is something I do want from you all."

They were all looking and waiting. I reckon they were ready to do or pay most anything. That's how things were handled.

"Damn it!" he said. "I want my five dollars back from that phony traffic ticket."

Long pause.

"That's all?"

"That's all. You give me my five dollars back and I'll give you back your receipt."

So they paid him the five dollars and he tore the receipt in two and they filed out of our house.

"You beat them, Daddy," I said. "You won!"

"That's right, boy," he told me. "And I taught them a very important lesson."

"What's that?" my mother asked, nervously.

"If they want to stop me now," he said, "they're going to have to kill me. And I don't think they've got the guts for it."

Then he laughed out loud. And so did I, not because it was funny, but because it seemed like the right thing to do at the time.

▶ **Final Check-in**

What do you think the mayor and his friends expected Mr. Garrett to ask for? Why do you suppose he only asked for his five dollars back? Do you think he did the right thing?

After You Read

A. Comprehension Check

1. The author admires his father for
  (1) knowing all about the law
  (2) making a lot of money
  (3) treating the kids to ice cream
  (4) standing up for what's right

2. Mr. Garrett thought the ticket was
  (1) phony
  (2) too expensive
  (3) deserved
  (4) forged

3. The town leaders harassed Mr. Garrett because he
  (1) was a lawyer
  (2) fought against racism
  (3) complained to the state legislature
  (4) refused to pay his ticket

4. Mr. Garrett beat the town leaders by
  (1) paying the ticket
  (2) refusing to represent people who resisted the Klan
  (3) proving that the town charter was illegal
  (4) fixing his taillights

B. Revisit the Reading Strategy
In this story, Mr. Garrett fought racism through the law. People have tried many other ways to overcome prejudice. In your experience, which of the ideas below would help most? Write **1** next to your first choice.

_____ Increase contact between people of different backgrounds.
_____ Provide job training for minorities.
_____ Have more minorities in Congress passing laws.

C. Think beyond the Reading
Think about these questions and discuss them with a partner. Answer the questions in writing if you wish.

1. The Ku Klux Klan used many forms of harassment against people who stood up to it. What would you do if you were harassed the way Mr. Garrett was?

2. Mr. Garrett believed that resisting the Klan was the right thing to do. Can you think of any situation that might have caused Mr. Garrett to stop resisting the Klan?

3. Is there anything so important to you that you would risk your life for it? If so, what?

Think About It: Identify Theme

You know that the topic of a story is what the story is about. The **theme** of the story is the message or major idea the author is expressing about the topic. It is a general message about life or human nature the writer wants to communicate.

For example, the topic of "The Right Thing to Do at the Time" is fighting for justice. The theme is that Garrett's father was right in doing whatever was necessary in the fight for justice. George Garrett states the theme of "The Right Thing to Do at the Time" in the opening paragraph:

> ▶ he would fight without stint, withholding nothing, offering no pity or quarter against what he took to be wrong—that is, against the untruth. He would go to any length he had to. And that is what this story is all about—how far one man would go to fight for the truth and against what was and is wrong.

In this story the theme is expressed primarily through the main character. Justice is so important to the main character that he's willing to risk his life and the lives of his family to defy the Ku Klux Klan.

A. Look at Theme

The theme of a story is usually not directly stated. More often, authors reveal the theme through the characters' actions and other details. Readers must be able to identify the theme as the story unfolds. Notice how Garrett develops his theme as he tells the story. What does this paragraph tell us?

> ▶ My father and his law partner were fighting against the Klan in court and in public with the promise that they would (as they, in fact, did) represent free of charge any person at all who chose to resist the Klan and wanted a lawyer.

We learn here that Garrett's father and his partner offered free legal representation to anyone who resisted the Klan. This further develops the theme that Garrett's father would do whatever was necessary to fight the Klan.

B. Practice Answer each question about theme.

1. Besides offering free legal representation, write three more things in the story that illustrate the theme.

   a. _____

   _____

   b. _____

   _____

   c. _____

   _____

2. State the theme of "The Right Thing to Do at the Time" in your own words by finishing this sentence.

   The theme of "The Right Thing to Do at the Time" _____

   _____

3. Now look back at "The Deli" in Lesson 1. Choose the statement below that best expresses its theme.
   (1) If you are naive, people will take advantage of you.
   (2) You can't trust teenagers who belong to gangs.
   (3) People will accept you if you treat them honestly and with respect.
   (4) If you don't stand up for your own rights, you may lose them.

 Talk About It
Racial inequality still exists in our society. Discuss with a group how you personally can take a stand for racial equality. Each group member should suggest at least two actions he or she can take. Anyone who has taken such a stand should tell the group about the experience.

Write About It: Write About an Incident

"The Right Thing to Do at the Time" describes an incident from George Garrett's childhood that taught him about standing up for what is right. Now you will have a chance to write about a time when you or someone you know stood up for a belief.

A. **Prewriting** Think of a time when you or someone you know had the opportunity to take a stand. Perhaps someone insulted you or a person you were with. Perhaps you or someone you know was being harassed or treated unfairly. Do you remember what happened? Choose a real-life situation and make notes by answering the following questions.

1. What happened?

2. When did it happen?

3. Who caused the problem?

4. What did they say or do?

5. What did you or someone you know say or do to take a stand?

6. How did it end?

7. Was the outcome satisfactory? Or should something different have been said or done? If so, what?

B. **Writing** On separate paper, write an account of the stand you or someone else took. Use your answers to the prewriting questions to explain what happened. Tell what the account is about and what happened. Explain whether you were satisfied with the outcome. Give details that support your conclusion.

▶ **Save your draft.** At the end of this unit, you will choose one of your drafts to work with further.

Life Skill: Read a Political Cartoon

The story "The Right Thing to Do at the Time" makes a point about racism in America. The political cartoon below deals with the same subject. Political cartoons often use humor to convey a serious message. They express the cartoonist's opinion about current political events.

For example, a cartoon might show a drawing of an elected official looking like a puppet, with strings attached to his hands and feet. The cartoonist might believe that the official does not think for himself, or that the official's actions are controlled by special interest groups.

Practice With a partner, study the cartoon and discuss it. Then answer the following questions.

1. To what group do the people burning the cross belong? _____

2. What does the woman want the Civil Rights Commission to do? _____
   _____

3. What does the man mean when he says, "That **is** the Civil Rights Commission"? _____
   _____

4. What does this cartoon have in common with the story "The Right Thing to Do at the Time"? _____

Lesson 5

LEARNING GOALS

Strategy: Predict content
Reading: Read biographical sketches
Skill: Compare and contrast
Writing: Write a biographical sketch
Life Skill: Read a map

Before You Read

The reading "Extraordinary People" consists of biographical sketches of two women in different parts of the world who took a stand to fight for what was right. A **biographical sketch** is a short article about a real person, briefly describing the major events or an important episode in the person's life. Magazine articles about real people are common examples of biographical sketches.

Before you read, **predict the content** of the two biographical sketches. What kind of information do you think you will find in a biographical sketch about a person who took a stand for what he or she believed in? Check each item below.

_____ place and year of birth   _____ family background   _____ nationality
_____ important beliefs   _____ injustices faced   _____ favorite song
_____ harassment suffered   _____ hobbies   _____ physical description

Preview the Reading

To preview "Extraordinary People," read the headings and look at the pictures. Who are the people these articles are about? What countries are they from?

Use the Strategy

Each biographical sketch tells about a woman who took great risks to fight for human rights in her native land. Each woman won the Nobel Peace Prize for the stand she took. As you read, predict what information will be in each sketch.

Extraordinary People

Herbert Buchsbaum

Rigoberta Menchú [b. 1960]

Rigoberta Menchú [ree goh BAIR tah main CHOO], a Quiché Maya Indian from the highlands of northern Guatemala, learned about injustice the hard way.

In September 1979, when she was 19, her younger brother was kidnapped by the Guatemalan army and accused of trying to help peasants win the right to own land. They tortured him brutally. Then he was marched to a village square where, in front of his family, he was doused with gasoline and set aflame.

Menchú at the United Nations

WIDE WORLD PHOTOS, INC.

A few months later, Menchú's father, who had also been arrested and tortured, led a peaceful protest to call attention to the peasants' grievances. The state security forces set fire to the building he was in, and he too was burned to death. A few weeks after that, the army arrested, tortured, and killed her mother. Menchú fled to Mexico, but vowed to continue the struggle where her parents left off. That was the first step on an extraordinary journey that would take a farm worker from a small village in Guatemala to the honor of the 1992 Nobel Peace Prize.[1]

Check-in ▶ What biographical facts have you learned about Menchú so far? What else do you predict you will learn about her life?

The oppression of Guatemala's native Maya peoples dates from 1524, when the tiny Central American country was conquered by Spain. Ever since, the Indian majority has been ruled by the Spanish-speaking minority, the *Ladinos,* most of whom are descended from the Spanish colonists.

In 1954, the military overthrew Guatemala's elected government and began a brutal war against the Indians. In the years since, 150,000 Indians have been killed, 1 million displaced,[2] and 50,000 made to "disappear."

In the late 1970s, as the repression[3] grew especially severe, some Indians began to resist. Menchú's family was among them.

---

1. **Nobel Peace Prize:** an annual prize established by Alfred B. Nobel, awarded for the encouragement of persons who work for the interests of humanity.
2. **displaced:** forced from one's homeland.
3. **repression:** unjust or cruel exercise of power.

Like many Indians, Menchú had become a farm laborer as a small child. As a teenager, Menchú began to teach herself to read and write Spanish, which would one day allow her to tell the story of her people to the outside world. Meanwhile, the Ladino land-owners, who had been taking land from peasants over the years, came one day to seize her home village. When her father tried to resist, he was arrested and tortured. The whole family was branded troublemakers, and the arrests began.

"The important thing is that what happened to me has happened to many other people too," Menchú writes in her autobiography. "My story is the story of all poor Guatemalans. My personal experience is the reality of a whole people."

While her suffering was typical, her resistance was not. In Mexico, Menchú continued to fight. She worked with international human rights groups and became a frequent visitor to the United Nations. There she was often seen walking the halls in her colorful native dress and bare feet, telling her story to the world.

Still, she remains a controversial figure in Guatemala, where government officials criticized her selection for the Nobel Prize. They accused her of supporting the country's guerrillas[4] and harming Guatemala's image abroad. Despite death threats if she returned, Menchú flew to the capital. Thousands of supporters lined the streets from the airport, cheering and shouting, "Viva Rigoberta!"

"I am overcome with emotion," she said. "I only wish that my parents could have been present."

---

4. guerrillas: independent fighting groups that use irregular methods to fight established governments.

◀ **Check-in**

Did you expect Menchú to return to her homeland? Did this sketch tell you everything you wanted to know about her life? Where could you find out more about her?

▶ **Update:** Since this article appeared, much has happened in Guatemala. In December 1996, a peace agreement between the army and the rebels was signed. Rigoberta Menchú was present at the signing.

Aung San Suu Kyi [b. 1944]

Sometimes what a person symbolizes can be more powerful than the person herself. Aung San Suu Kyi [AWNG SAHN SOO CHEE], a writer, was not seen nor heard in public from the time she was arrested on July 20, 1989, until her release from house arrest in 1995. Yet during that time she represented the hope of all those who oppose the brutal government of Myanmar, where she was held prisoner.

Suu Kyi addressing her followers

Herald Journal AP/WIDE WORLD

Suu Kyi became the hero of Myanmar's struggle for democracy partly by chance and partly by fate. She is the daughter of Aung San, a legendary general who helped lead Myanmar (then known as Burma)[5] to independence from British colonial rule in the 1940s. In 1946, when Suu Kyi was 2 years old, the general was gunned down by a rival faction.

In 1962, a military dictatorship seized power, declaring war against the country's ethnic minorities. In attempts to "purify" the nation, the army looted and burned some 850 rural villages, raped several thousand women, killed and tortured thousands, enslaved hundreds of young boys, and forced more than a million refugees to flee their homes, according to a United Nations report.

But as Myanmar plunged into poverty and civil war, Suu Kyi was living comfortably in England with her British husband and their two sons. In 1988, she received news from Yangon, the nation's capital (formerly Rangoon), that her mother was gravely ill. She immediately packed a suitcase and flew home. As she slept by her mother's side, a protest movement among the nation's students began to pick up steam.

At first Suu Kyi stayed out of the fray. But after a massacre that August, in which thousands of protesters were killed, she could no longer keep silent. "This was not a time when anyone who cares can stay out," she said then. "As my father's daughter, I felt I had a duty to get involved." When she spoke, half a million people came to listen. The speech, which advocated a nonviolent "revolution of

---

5. Burma: The military government changed the country's name to Myanmar. However, Aung San Suu Kyi and her supporters continue to use the name Burma for their native land.

the spirit," electrified the nation and established her as leader of the struggle for democracy and human rights.

What facts have you learned about Suu Kyi so far? Does Suu Kyi remind you of Rigoberta Menchú? In what ways? What else do you think you will learn about Suu Kyi?

◀ Check-in

As she began to campaign around the country, the army fought back with bullets. Once, in April 1989, she was walking down the street with a group of supporters when a squad of soldiers jumped from a jeep, knelt, and prepared to fire. Suu Kyi motioned her companions away and marched straight up to the riflemen. "It seemed so much simpler to provide them with a single target than to bring everyone else in," she said later. The soldiers withdrew.

In July 1989, she was placed under "house arrest," forbidden to leave her home or have any contact with the outside world, including her family in England. Her house was surrounded by tanks and barbed wire. Soldiers with bayonets were stationed outside. She was not allowed out until she was released from house arrest in 1995.

But her imprisonment did not stop her party from winning a landslide election in 1990, making her the nation's legally elected leader. And it didn't keep her from winning the Nobel Peace Prize in 1991. The army, which had ignored the election results, offered her the chance to travel to Norway to accept the prize if she promised never to return. She refused.

Her father, until he was killed, had always said he expected to make whatever sacrifice his struggle required. "My only concern," said Suu Kyi, "is that I prove worthy of him."

▶ **Final Check-in**
On page 56, you predicted you would find certain information in the biographical sketches. Did your predictions help you to better understand the sketches? In what ways?

▶ **Update:** Upon release from house arrest in 1995, Suu Kyi continued to lead the opposition against the brutal military regime that controlled her country. In public speeches, she read lists of activists who were imprisoned by the government. On December 4, 1996, she was again placed under house arrest.

After You Read

A. Comprehension Check

1. What cause did Rigoberta Menchú fight for? _____

2. Why did she flee to Mexico? _____

3. In what year did Menchú win the Nobel Peace Prize? _____

4. What happened when Menchú returned to Guatemala after winning the prize? _____

   _____

5. What event led Aung San Suu Kyi to join the fight against the government of

   Myanmar? _____

6. What cause was Suu Kyi fighting for? _____

7. What happened to Suu Kyi in July 1989? _____

   _____

8. Why did Suu Kyi not go to Norway to accept the Nobel Peace Prize? _____

   _____

B. Revisit the Reading Strategy
Before reading the two biographical sketches, you predicted what you expected to find in them. Which of your predictions were included in these sketches? Write two other things that you learned that you didn't know before.

_____

_____

C. Think beyond the Reading
Think about these questions and discuss them with a partner. Answer them in writing if you wish.

1. What do you think Menchú's childhood experiences taught her about her country's government?

2. Aung San Suu Kyi left her family in England to fight for freedom in Myanmar. Do you approve of her decision? Why or why not?

Think About It: Compare and Contrast

When you **compare** things, you look for how they are alike or similar.
When you **contrast** them, you notice how they are different. The two
biographical sketches you read contain both similarities and differences.

For example, you can compare the actions of Rigoberta Menchú and Aung
San Suu Kyi: they both risked their lives to fight for freedom for their
people. You can contrast their upbringings: Menchú was a Guatemalan
farm worker, and Suu Kyi is the daughter of a general from Myanmar.

A. Look at Comparing and Contrasting

Look at the comparison and contrast chart below for the two women
you read about. For comparisons, information is listed under the
column headed **Both.** Contrasting information is listed under each
woman's name.

Comparison and Contrast of Menchú and Suu Kyi

Topic	Menchú	Suu Kyi	Both
Gender			female
When born	1960	1944	
Where born	Guatemala	Burma (now Myanmar)	

For the first topic, the gender is filled in under the heading **Both**
because they're both female. That's a comparison. For the second topic,
their dates of birth are filled in under each name because they were
born in different years. That's a contrast. The same is true for the third
topic, **Where born.**

B. Practice Fill in the comparison and contrast chart below. The first topic is completed for you.

Comparison and Contrast of Menchú and Suu Kyi

Topic	Menchú	Suu Kyi	Both
Form of government they opposed			military dictatorship
Former colonial ruler			
Risks they took			
What they were resisting			
What they were fighting for			
When they won Nobel Peace Prize			

▶ **Talk About It**

Summarize one of the biographical sketches. When you summarize, you cover just the main points without much detail. First, reread the sketch and take notes on the most important points. Then with a partner, take turns telling your summaries.

Write About It: Write a Biographical Sketch

The biographical sketches in "Extraordinary People" describe the heroism of two people who rose to remarkable challenges. Think of someone you know who has taken a stand. Maybe you know someone who took part in the Civil Rights movement of the 1960s. Or perhaps you know someone who is fighting now for a cause in your community or who took a stand against some type of abuse. Write a brief biographical sketch describing that person.

A. **Prewriting** After you decide on someone to write about, you'll need to interview that person. Start by making a list of questions to ask. Here are some examples. Add other questions you want answered.

1. When and where were you born?

2. What stand did you take?

3. Where did this take place?

4. What made you decide to take a stand?

5. What did you do to take a stand?

6. How did you feel? Were you scared?

7. What were the results of your actions?

8. Looking back, how do you feel about what you did? Would you do it again?

Write your questions on separate paper, leaving enough space between them to take notes during your interview. Then interview the person.

B. **Writing** Write a biographical sketch that includes the most interesting answers to the questions you asked. Begin by telling who the sketch is about and what the person stood up for. Close by saying whether the person would take the stand again, and why.

▶ **Save your draft.** At the end of this unit, you will choose one of your drafts to work with further.

Life Skill: Read a Map

Rigoberta Menchú's home country, Guatemala, is in Central America, a bridge of land that connects North and South America. You can use a map to find where she lives. A **map** is a representation that shows the major features of an area. There are maps of cities, states, countries, the world, and even the stars. A map usually shows the boundaries of separate places in the area and gives the names of important features. Directions are labeled with letters: *N* for north, *S* for south, *E* for east, and *W* for west.

The map below shows Rigoberta Menchú's home country of Guatemala and other Central American countries, plus Mexico and Cuba.

Practice Answer these questions.

1. What countries border on Guatemala? _____

   _____

2. What body of water is east of Guatemala? _____

3. What body of water is west of Guatemala? _____

Lesson 6

LEARNING GOALS

Strategy: Use your prior knowledge
Reading: Read part of a speech
Skill: Identify the main idea and details
Writing: Write an opinion
Life Skill: Read a line graph

Before You Read

"I Have a Dream" is a very famous speech that the Reverend Martin Luther King, Jr., gave at a huge civil rights rally in Washington, D.C., in 1963. Dr. King worked all his life to bring racial equality to Americans. He was assassinated in 1968, at age 39. Before you read the speech, use your **prior knowledge** to list three things you already know about Dr. King.

_____

_____

_____

Preview the Reading

To preview the excerpt from "I Have a Dream," look at the picture. Read the title and the first paragraph aloud. What does Dr. King say he has?

AP/WIDE WORLD PHOTOS

► **Use the Strategy**
In "I Have a Dream," Martin Luther King, Jr., moved a nation with his vision of an America that truly offers equal opportunity for all. As you read the excerpt below, think about Dr. King's views. Do you share them? Or do your views differ? If so, in what ways?

from I Have a Dream

Martin Luther King, Jr.

So I say to you, my friends, that even though we must face the difficulties of today and tomorrow, I still have a dream. It is a dream deeply rooted in the American dream that one day this nation will rise up and live out the true meaning of its creed[1]—we hold these truths to be self-evident, that all men are created equal.

Check-in

"We hold these truths to be self-evident, that all men are created equal." Dr. King quoted this sentence from an important document written in 1776. Do you know which document?

I have a dream that one day on the red hills of Georgia, sons of former slaves and sons of former slave-owners will be able to sit down together at the table of brotherhood.

I have a dream that one day, even the state of Mississippi, a state sweltering with the heat of injustice, sweltering with the heat of oppression, will be transformed into an oasis of freedom and justice.

I have a dream my four little children will one day live in a nation where they will not be judged by the color of their skin but by the content of their character. I have a dream today!

I have a dream that one day, down in Alabama, with its vicious racists, with its governor[2] having his lips dripping with the words of interposition[3] and nullification,[4] that one day, right there in Alabama, little black boys and black girls will be able to join hands with little white boys and white girls as sisters and brothers. I have a dream today!

---

1. **creed:** set of beliefs to live by.
2. **governor:** refers to George Wallace, who was governor of Alabama at the time.
3. **interposition:** a state putting its own authority before the authority of the federal government.
4. **nullification:** the action of a state trying to prevent enforcement of federal law.

I have a dream that one day every valley shall be exalted, every hill and mountain shall be made low, the rough places shall be made plain, and the crooked places shall be made straight and the glory of the Lord will be revealed and all flesh shall see it together.

This is our hope. This is the faith that I go back to the South with.

With this faith we will be able to hear out of the mountain of despair a stone of hope. With this faith we will be able to transform the jangling discords of our nation into a beautiful symphony of brotherhood.

With this faith we will be able to work together, to pray together, to struggle together, to go to jail together, to stand up for freedom together, knowing that we will be free one day. This will be the day when all of God's children will be able to sing with new meaning— "my country 'tis of thee; sweet land of liberty; of thee I sing; land where my fathers died, land of the pilgrim's pride; from every mountain side, let freedom ring"—and if America is to be a great nation, this must become true.

So let freedom ring from the prodigious hilltops of New Hampshire.

Let freedom ring from the mighty mountains of New York.

Let freedom ring from the heightening Alleghenies of Pennsylvania.

Let freedom ring from the snow-capped Rockies of Colorado.

Let freedom ring from the curvaceous slopes of California.

But not only that.

Let freedom ring from Stone Mountain of Georgia.

Let freedom ring from Lookout Mountain of Tennessee.

Let freedom ring from every hill and molehill of Mississippi, from every mountainside, let freedom ring.

And when we allow freedom to ring, when we let it ring from every village and hamlet, from every state and city, we will be able to speed up that day when all of God's children—black men and white men, Jews and Gentiles, Catholics and Protestants—will be able to join hands and to sing in the words of the old Negro spiritual, "Free at last, free at last; thank God Almighty, we are free at last."

▶ **Final Check-in**

Did your prior knowledge of Dr. King and the Civil Rights movement of the 1960s help you to read and respond to Dr. King's impassioned plea? How do you think people would react to this speech today?

After You Read

A. Comprehension Check

1. According to Dr. King, America's creed is that
(1) everyone should have a dream
(2) all men are created equal
(3) God is with us
(4) we are free at last

2. What phrase is repeated many times throughout the speech?
(1) This is our hope.
(2) All men are created equal.
(3) Free at last.
(4) I have a dream.

3. Dr. King hopes his children will be judged by
(1) the color of their skin
(2) the content of their character
(3) the fact that their father is a minister
(4) where they live

4. What is Dr. King's impassioned plea in this speech?
(1) to increase people's prejudices
(2) to found a separate black nation
(3) to let freedom ring
(4) to admit that freedom is only a dream

B. Revisit the Reading Strategy
Based on what you already knew and what you learned from reading part of Dr. King's speech, which statements below do you think he would have agreed with? Disagreed with?

Agree   Disagree

_____   _____   **1.** The way to equality is harmony among all God's children.

_____   _____   **2.** Religion is just a tool to make people less angry.

_____   _____   **3.** The divisions between the races can never be bridged.

C. Think beyond the Reading
Think about these questions and discuss them with a partner. Answer the questions in writing if you wish.

1. What leaders today, if any, do you think are carrying on Dr. King's work?

2. Martin Luther King knew he risked his life for his beliefs. How do you think he found the courage to speak out?

3. Martin Luther King was murdered for standing up and speaking out for freedom and equality for all people. Do you think the price he paid was worth it? Why or why not?

Think About It: Identify the Main Idea and Details

As you learned in Lesson 3, the **main idea** of a piece of writing is its most important point—its central thought or meaning. Sometimes it is stated in the first sentence, but it can be anywhere in a piece of writing. Sometimes the main idea is not stated directly, so you have to figure it out from the reading as a whole. Sometimes, as in Dr. King's speech, it is stated many times.

Whether the main idea is stated or implied, the job of the **supporting details** is to give specific facts, examples, or reasons to support or explain the main idea.

A. Look at Main Idea and Details

The main idea of the paragraph below is that the author still has a dream. Notice how the details support that idea.

▶ So I say to you, my friends, that even though we must face the difficulties of today and tomorrow, I still have a dream. It is a dream deeply rooted in the American dream that one day this nation will rise up and live out the true meaning of its creed—we hold these truths to be self-evident, that all men are created equal.

Main Idea		
I still have a dream.		
Detail	**Detail**	**Detail**
The dream is deeply rooted in the American dream.	One day the nation will rise up.	The nation will live out its creed: All men are created equal.

B. Practice

1. Read the excerpt below. Then list five details from the excerpt.

> ▶ With this faith we will be able to work together, to pray together, to struggle together, to go to jail together, to stand up for freedom together, knowing that we will be free one day.

_____

_____

_____

Are the details you listed facts, examples, or reasons? _____

2. Read the excerpt below and answer the questions that follow.

> ▶ So let freedom ring from the prodigious hilltops of New Hampshire.
> Let freedom ring from the mighty mountains of New York.
> Let freedom ring from the heightening Alleghenies of Pennsylvania.
> Let freedom ring from the snow-capped Rockies of Colorado.
> Let freedom ring from the curvaceous slopes of California.
> But not only that.
> Let freedom ring from Stone Mountain of Georgia.
> Let freedom ring from Lookout Mountain of Tennessee.
> Let freedom ring from every hill and molehill of Mississippi, from every mountainside, let freedom ring.

   a. What is the main idea of this excerpt? _____

   b. What do all the details have in common? _____

   _____

3. Reread the whole excerpt of Dr. King's speech. Then in your own words, write the main idea of the whole passage.

   _____

▶ **Talk About It**
In a small group, take turns reading sections of the speech aloud. Practice making dramatic pauses and hand gestures. If you've seen the film of Dr. King delivering this speech, try to match his tone of voice.

Write About It: Write an Opinion

Martin Luther King, Jr., gave his "I Have a Dream" speech in 1963. This speech established the direction of the Civil Rights movement for years to come. However, people have different opinions about whether the dream of equality has been realized. Do you think Dr. King's dream has come true? Write your opinion.

A. **Prewriting** To decide whether you feel that Dr. King's dream of equality has come true, think about the examples of freedom and equality that he gave in his speech. How many of them are true today? Think of other examples of equality and inequality that you know of, too. Use the idea map below to organize your thoughts. Fill in the blanks with facts, examples, or reasons that support your opinion.

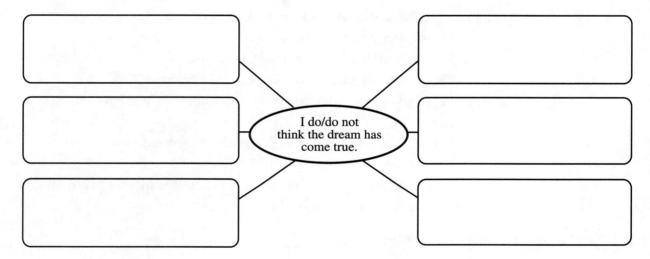

B. **Writing** Write your opinion using the items on your idea map. Use the central statement from the idea map as your topic sentence. Add facts, examples, or reasons as details to support your opinion. You can write everything in one paragraph, or you can put each supporting detail in a separate paragraph.

▶ **Save your draft.** At the end of this unit, you will choose one of your drafts to work with further.

Life Skill: Read a Line Graph

As you learned in Lesson 3, graphs are used in place of words to display certain kinds of information. **Line graphs** are especially helpful for showing changes over a period of time. To understand a line graph, first read the title and the labels along the side and the bottom. The labels show what the numbers stand for.

Practice Study the line graph below and answer the questions that follow. Note that the total number of members of Congress is 535 every year.

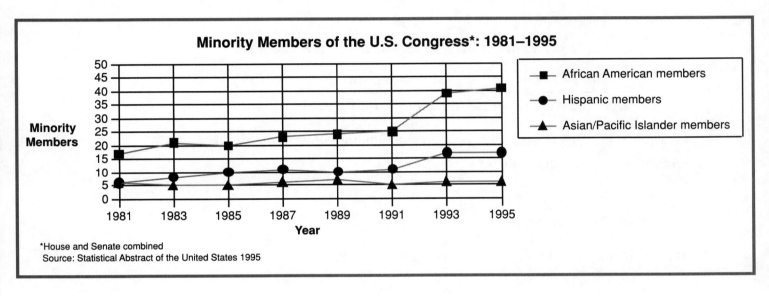

Minority Members of the U.S. Congress*: 1981–1995

*House and Senate combined
Source: Statistical Abstract of the United States 1995

1. What is the graph about? _____

2. About how many African American members of Congress were there in 1981? _____

3. About how many African American legislators were there in 1995? _____

4. In 1981, minority members made up 5 percent of Congress. By 1995, they made up 12 percent of Congress. What is the trend in the number of minority legislators? _____

   _____

5. Which minority group has maintained a fairly steady representation? _____

   _____

Writing Skills Mini-Lesson:
Commas in Compound Sentences

Use a comma to separate the simple sentences in a **compound sentence,**
but do not use a comma in a **compound subject** or **compound verb.**

1. **Compound sentences.** A compound sentence has two parts. Each part
   is a complete thought and has its own subject and verb. You join the two
   parts with a connecting word like *and, or, but, yet,* or *so.* Use a comma
   before the connecting word.

   > Subject Verb   Subject Verb
   > Some people want new leaders, **so** they vote for new candidates.

   > Subject Verb   Subject Verb
   > Some people want new leaders, **but** they refuse to vote.

2. **Compound subjects and verbs.** Two subjects joined with the word
   and make a compound subject.

   > Compound
   > Subject   Verb
   > **Men and women** register before an election.

   Two verbs joined with *and* make a compound verb.

   > Compound
   > Subject Verb
   > People **go and vote** on election day.

   Do not use a comma before *and* in a compound subject or verb.

Practice Copy the paragraph, adding commas where necessary.

> My family always reads and talks about the news. We discuss and
> even argue about politics. My mother and father have voted in every
> election since 1968. My brother voted four years ago but I was too
> young to vote then. I turned 18 last year and I voted for the first time.
> My sister and I registered to vote on the same day. We all voted in the
> next election but we voted for different people. My mother and father
> voted for the Democratic candidate. My sister and brother voted for
> the Republican candidate and I voted for an independent. My
> candidate lost but I was still excited about voting for the first time.

Reading Review

The Woman Who Conquered the Klan ▬▬▬

Beulah Mae Donald was a quiet, unassuming woman who dropped out of school at age 15. She spent the next 46 years raising and supporting her eight children. They made her proud by going to college and getting good jobs. Her youngest son, Michael, was a shy, sweet young man. At 19, he was a college student who worked part-time at the local newspaper.

One night in March 1981, Michael was accosted by two white men in his hometown of Mobile, Alabama. They dragged him off the street at gunpoint and killed him, then strung his body from a tree. The killers were members of the Ku Klux Klan. The next morning, the Great Titan of the Klan called a TV station and said, "That's a pretty sight. Gonna look good on the news."

The district attorney claimed that race was not a factor in the murder. He suspected it was drug-related, so Ms. Donald let them search Michael's room. They found nothing. The local authorities found no suspects, and neither did the FBI. The case was closed.

Ms. Donald had to know what had happened. She wanted to prove that "Michael did no wrong." The family organized a march and picketed the courthouse but got no action. Finally, six months after the murder, the FBI reopened its investigation. In January 1985, Klansman James (Tiger) Knowles went to prison for life and Klansman Henry Hays was sentenced to death. Ms. Donald did not attend the trial because she couldn't bear to look at the men who had murdered her son.

Then, in 1987, the Southern Poverty Law Center suggested bringing a civil suit against the Klan. They thought they could prove conspiracy. The Klan offered to settle for $100,000. Ms. Donald refused. She wanted to avenge her son's death by breaking the Klan—and she did. The landmark case made the Klan itself financially responsible for the criminal activities of any member. The jury awarded Ms. Donald $7 million. The branch of the Klan that killed her son didn't have that much money, so now it's penniless. No amount of money can take away the family's pain, but it brings them some satisfaction to know they may have crippled that branch of the Klan for good.

Choose the best answer for each question.

1. The main idea of the article is that
   (1) Beulah Mae Donald had eight children
   (2) Beulah Mae Donald fought the Klan and won
   (3) the authorities didn't take Michael's death seriously
   (4) the Klan wanted TV coverage of the lynching

2. The first time the FBI investigated Michael Donald's murder,
   (1) they solved the case
   (2) they knew it was drug-related
   (3) they found no suspects
   (4) they knew it was a racist crime

3. Beulah Mae Donald is like Rigoberta Menchú in that
   (1) she traveled to a foreign country
   (2) she lost a family member to the Klan
   (3) she lived in the American South
   (4) she stood up for what was right

4. Beulah Mae Donald is different from Mr. Garrett in that
   (1) she fought against the Klan
   (2) she lived in the South
   (3) she stood up for what was right
   (4) she raised eight children

Writing Process

In Unit 2, you wrote three first drafts. Choose the piece that you would like to work with further. You will revise, edit, and make a final copy of this draft.

_____ your paragraph about a time when you or someone you know took a stand (page 54)

_____ your biographical sketch about someone who took a stand (page 64)

_____ your opinion about Dr. King's dream coming true (page 72)

Find the first draft of your choice. Then turn to page 159 in this book. Follow steps 3, 4, and 5 in the Writing Process to create a final draft.

As you revise, check your draft for these specific points:

Paragraph about taking a stand: Make sure you use details to describe the stand.

Biographical sketch: Be sure you include how and why the person took the stand.

Your opinion about King's dream: Be sure you include details that support your opinion.

Unit 3 Relationships

Relationships are the bonds between people. You form relationships with many people during your lifetime: with your family, your friends, your neighbors, and your co-workers. Good relationships can help make your life more fulfilling. But good relationships don't just happen. To have good relationships, people must care about one another and be willing to share each other's lives. In Unit 3, you will read about relationships between parents and children in two different families. You will also read some graphs that reveal how relationships in the U.S. have been changing over the last half century.

Before you begin Unit 3, think about the relationships in your life. Which are most important to you? Which have helped to shape your life?

▶ **Be an Active Reader**

As you read the selections in this unit
- Put a question mark (?) by things you do not understand.
- Underline words you do not know. Try to use context clues to figure them out.

After you read each selection in this unit
- Reread sections you marked with a question mark (?). If they still do not make sense, discuss them with a partner or your instructor.
- Look at words you underlined. Discuss any words you still don't understand with a partner or your instructor, or look them up in a dictionary.

Lesson 7

LEARNING GOALS

Strategy: Visualize
Reading: Read a scene from a play
Skill: Make inferences
Writing: Write dialogue
Life Skill: Read a map

Before You Read

In this lesson, you will read an excerpt from the play *On Golden Pond*. The play explores the relationships among a husband, a wife, and their adult daughter.

Reading a play is different from reading a novel or short story. Plays do not include long passages that describe the characters, the settings, or the actions. A brief description of the setting and a listing of the cast of characters is usually provided, but most of what you read are the words the characters speak, called *dialogue*. The name of the character speaking precedes each line of dialogue. Stage directions are usually in italics set apart by parentheses. They are not meant to be spoken. They tell the actors where to move or how to speak. Look at this example of dialogue:

ETHEL: Sit down and tell me about your trip.

CHELSEA: (*An outburst*) I don't want to sit down.

Can you tell which line is spoken by Ethel and which is spoken by Chelsea? Can you visualize how the actress might portray "an outburst"? If you were playing the part of Chelsea, how would you speak this line?

When you read a play, it is important to try to **visualize** the characters, their actions, and the setting. Picture what the action on the stage looks like as the characters speak their lines.

Preview the Reading

Preview the scene by skimming through it. Read the characters' names. Look at the photos from the movie that was based on this play.

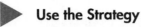

▶ **Use the Strategy**
As you read, pay attention to which character is speaking each line.
Use the stage directions to help you visualize what is going on.

from On Golden Pond

Ernest Thompson

PHOTOFEST

**Katharine Hepburn plays Ethel and Jane Fonda plays Chelsea
in the 1981 movie version of *On Golden Pond*.**

*In this play, Norman and Ethel Thayer, an elderly married
couple, are spending the summer in their home on Golden Pond
in the woods of Maine. Chelsea, their adult daughter, is visiting
for the first time in eight years. Chelsea has had troubled
relationships with her parents. In the first scene, Chelsea has
arrived earlier in the day. She and her mother are in the living
room. Chelsea is standing and Ethel is sitting in a chair.*

CHELSEA: (*Turning to the mantel and picking up a picture*) Look
at this. Chelsea on the swim team. That was a great
exercise in humiliation.

ETHEL: Oh, stop it. You were a good diver.

CHELSEA: I wasn't a good diver. I was a good sport. I could
never do a damn back flip.

ETHEL: Well, we were proud of you for trying.

CHELSEA: Right. Everyone got a big splash out of me trying.
Why do you think I subjected myself to all that? I

wasn't aiming for the 1956 Olympics, you know. I was just trying to please Norman. Because he'd been a diver, in the eighteen hundreds.

ETHEL: Can't you be home for five minutes without getting started on the past?

CHELSEA: This house seems to set me off.

ETHEL: Well, it shouldn't. It's a nice house.

CHELSEA: I act like a big person everywhere else. I do. I'm in charge in Los Angeles. I guess I've never grown up on Golden Pond. Do you understand?

ETHEL: I don't think so.

CHELSEA: It doesn't matter. There's just something about coming back here that makes me feel like a little fat girl.

ETHEL: Sit down and tell me about your trip.

CHELSEA: (*An outburst*) I don't want to sit down. Where were you all that time? You never bailed me out.

ETHEL: I didn't know you needed bailing out.

CHELSEA: Well, I did.

ETHEL: Here we go again. You had a miserable childhood. Your father was overbearing, your mother ignored you. What else is new? Don't you think everyone looks back on their childhood with some bitterness or regret about something? You are a big girl now, aren't you tired of it all? You have this unpleasant chip on your shoulder which is very unattractive. You only come home when I beg you to, and when you get here all you can do is be disagreeable about the past. Life marches by, Chelsea, I suggest you get on with it. (*ETHEL stands and glares at CHELSEA*) You're such a nice person. Can't you think of something nice to say?

When you read Ethel's stage direction above, did you picture the action? What did Ethel do? How did she look?

◀ Check-in

CHELSEA: I married Bill in Brussels.

ETHEL: You did what in Brussels?

CHELSEA: I married Bill.

ETHEL: Does it count in this country?

CHELSEA: 'Fraid so.

ETHEL: (*Stepping to* CHELSEA *and kissing her*) Well, bless you. Congratulations.

CHELSEA: Thank you.

ETHEL: You have an odd way of building up to good news.

CHELSEA: I know.

Later in the same scene, Norman is standing and gazing out at the pond. Chelsea walks over and sits down near him. They have the following conversation.

Katharine Hepburn, Henry Fonda, and Jane Fonda in *On Golden Pond*.

NORMAN: Did you hear what the stupid Yankees did?

CHELSEA: No. (*Carefully*) I don't want to talk about baseball.

NORMAN: Oh. I was just going to mention something you might have found interesting, but it doesn't matter.

CHELSEA: I want to talk about us.

NORMAN: What about us?

CHELSEA: You want to sit down?

NORMAN: (*Nervous*) Should I? . . . Perhaps I'd better stand.

CHELSEA: (*Smiling*) I just wanted to say . . . that I'm sorry.

NORMAN: Fine. No problem.

CHELSEA: Don't you want to know what I'm sorry about?

NORMAN: I suppose so.

CHELSEA: Um. I'm sorry that our communication has been so bad. That my . . . that I've been walking around with a chip on my shoulder.

NORMAN: Oh.

CHELSEA: I'm sorry I didn't come to your retirement dinner.

NORMAN: Oh. That was some time ago, you know.

CHELSEA: Yes. I know.

NORMAN: Well, you really missed something there. I gave them quite a speech.

CHELSEA: I heard about it. I heard you were very funny.

NORMAN: I was. I was a scream.

CHELSEA: I'm sorry I missed it.

NORMAN: Well . . .

CHELSEA: Um, I think it would be a good idea if we tried . . . to have the kind of relationship we're supposed to have.

NORMAN: What kind of relationship are we supposed to have?

CHELSEA: Um. Like a father and a daughter.

NORMAN: Ah. Well. Just in the nick of time, huh?

CHELSEA: No.

NORMAN: Worried about the will, are you? I'm leaving everything to you, except what I'm taking with me.

CHELSEA: Stop it. (*She steps to him*) I don't want anything. We've been mad at each other for too long.

NORMAN: Oh. I didn't realize we were mad. I thought we just didn't like each other.

CHELSEA: I want to be your friend.

NORMAN: Oh. Okay. Does this mean you're going to come around more often? I may not last eight more years, you know.

CHELSEA: Tsk. I'll come around more often.

NORMAN: Well. It would mean a lot to your mother.

CHELSEA: Okay. (*They look at each other a moment, nothing more to say*) Now you want to tell me about the Yankees?

NORMAN: The Yankees? They're bums.

▶ **Final Check-in**

Visualize the expressions on Norman's and Chelsea's faces at the end of this scene. How do you think they look?

After You Read

A. Comprehension Check

1. Why did Chelsea join the swim team in high school?
   (1) to lose weight
   (2) to please her father
   (3) to attract boys
   (4) to learn to do a back flip

2. Ethel thinks her daughter should
   (1) avoid Norman
   (2) marry Bill
   (3) start swimming again
   (4) put the past behind her

3. How do you think Chelsea feels about her father?
   (1) She loves him.
   (2) She's afraid of him.
   (3) She never wants to see him again.
   (4) She's ashamed of him.

4. Norman talks to his daughter about baseball because
   (1) he used to play in the major leagues
   (2) he doesn't know what else to say
   (3) he's a big Yankees fan
   (4) he wants to teach her to play

B. Revisit the Reading Strategy
Reading a play is different from reading a story because it leaves so much to your imagination. List some of the things you visualized as you read these scenes. Did you visualize how the Thayers' home on Golden Pond looks? How the characters looked? The expressions on their faces? Discuss your ideas with the group.

_____

_____

C. Think beyond the Reading
Think about these questions and discuss them with a partner. Answer the questions in writing if you wish.

1. Like Chelsea's family, many parents and children expect different things from each other. What did your parents expect from you when you were young? How did they expect you to act? What kind of job did they want you to have? How did your ideas about your life differ from theirs?

2. If you are a parent, what do you expect from your children? How do you want them to act toward you? How do their ideas differ from yours?

Think About It: Make Inferences

When you **make inferences,** you use your own experience and knowledge to understand ideas that aren't stated in words. Inferring involves using clues and reading between the lines to figure things out. What can you infer about the relationship between Chelsea and Norman from this dialogue?

> NORMAN: Does this mean you're going to come around more often? I may not last eight more years, you know.
>
> CHELSEA: Tsk. I'll come around more often.
>
> NORMAN: Well. It would mean a lot to your mother.

You can infer from this that Chelsea has not visited her parents in eight years, and that her father misses her but he won't admit it.

A. Look at Inferences

In the passage that follows, use your own experience to fill in the missing pieces. What can you infer about Chelsea's relationship with her parents?

> CHELSEA: Why do you think I subjected myself to all that? I wasn't aiming for the 1956 Olympics, you know. I was just trying to please Norman. Because he'd been a diver, in the eighteen hundreds.
>
> ETHEL: Can't you be home for five minutes without getting started on the past?

You may infer that Chelsea spent her youth trying to please her father and still resents him. Her sarcasm about how long ago he was a diver shows that she still feels anger about it. You can also infer that Ethel gets impatient with Chelsea's self-pity, and that they've had similar discussions in the past.

B. Practice
Read the passages and answer the questions. Use your own experience as well as the clues in the lines.

1. ▶ CHELSEA: (*An outburst*) I don't want to sit down. Where were you all that time? You never bailed me out.

   ETHEL: I didn't know you needed bailing out.

   CHELSEA: Well, I did.

   ETHEL: Here we go again. You had a miserable childhood. Your father was overbearing, your mother ignored you. What else is new? Don't you think everyone looks back on their childhood with some bitterness or regret about something? You are a big girl now, aren't you tired of it all? You have this unpleasant chip on your shoulder which is very unattractive. You only come home when I beg you to, and when you get here all you can do is be disagreeable about the past. Life marches by, Chelsea, I suggest you get on with it. (*Ethel stands and glares at Chelsea*) You're such a nice person. Can't you think of something nice to say?

a. What can you infer about Ethel's feelings toward Chelsea? _____

_____

b. What can you infer about Chelsea and Ethel's relationship when Chelsea was growing

up? _____

2. ▶ NORMAN: Did you hear what the stupid Yankees did?

  CHELSEA: No. (*Carefully*) I don't want to talk about baseball.

  NORMAN: Oh. I was just going to mention something you might have found
      interesting, but it doesn't matter.

  CHELSEA: I want to talk about us.

  NORMAN: What about us?

  CHELSEA: You want to sit down?

  NORMAN: (*Nervous*) Should I? . . . Perhaps I'd better stand.

  CHELSEA: (*Smiling*) I just wanted to say . . . that I'm sorry.

  NORMAN: Fine. No problem.

  CHELSEA: Don't you want to know what I'm sorry about?

  NORMAN: I suppose so.

  CHELSEA: Um. I'm sorry that our communication has been so bad.
      That my . . . that I've been walking around with a chip on my shoulder.

  NORMAN: Oh.

a. What can you infer about Chelsea's feelings toward Norman? _____

_____

b. What can you infer about Norman's attitude toward discussing feelings? _____

_____

▶ **Talk About It**
In groups of three, play the roles of Chelsea, Ethel, and Norman. Follow the stage directions and read the lines as you picture the characters would say them.

Write About It: Write Dialogue

Plays consist mostly of dialogue. Try writing a brief piece of dialogue yourself. First think of two characters, the relationship between them, and a situation. Examples might be a parent and child arguing over bedtime, or a discussion between two friends.

A. Prewriting List the two characters you will include in the dialogue. Write a sentence or two to describe the situation. Then make a word map of the important phrases the two characters will say to each other, in order. The word map below shows what a parent and child might say to each other at bedtime.

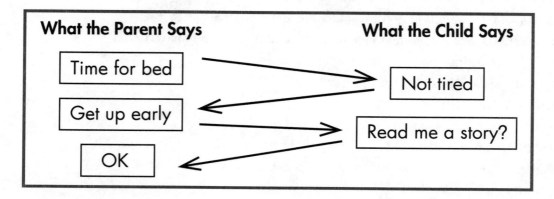

Read this sample dialogue based on the word map above. Each phrase from the word map makes a line of dialogue. Read the sample dialogue.

> LARRY: Alana, honey, it's time for bed.
> ALANA: Oh, Daddy, I don't want to. I'm not tired.
> LARRY: You will be when you have to get up early for school.
> ALANA: Please, please, please read me a story.
> LARRY: (*Giving in*) Okay, sweetie. But brush your teeth first.

B. Writing On separate paper, use your word map to write your own dialogue.

▶ **Save your draft.** At the end of this unit, you will choose one of your drafts to work with further.

Life Skill: Read a Map

Imagine that it is your turn to host a family get-together, and you have recently moved to a town named Rector. Your relatives will be driving from various locations. You decide to send everyone the map below so they can find their way to Rector.

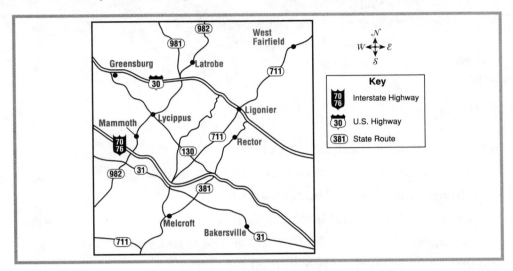

Practice On your own or with a partner, study the map. Find Rector. Then answer the questions.

1. What route is Rector on? _____

2. If you were driving north on Route 381 from Melcroft to Rector, what major highway

   would you cross? _____

3. If you were driving from Lycippus, what two roads would take you most directly to

   Rector? _____

4. If you were driving from West Fairfield, what three roads would take you most directly to

   Rector? _____

5. What direction is Rector from Ligonier?
   (1) north   (2) east   (3) south   (4) west

6. What direction is Rector from Mammoth?
   (1) north   (2) east   (3) south   (4) west

7. If you were driving home to Bakersville at sunset, would the sun be in your eyes? _____

Lesson 8

LEARNING GOALS

Strategy: Imagine
Reading: Read a story
Skill: Identify theme
Writing: Write a friendly letter
Life Skill: Read a family tree

Before You Read

"The Corn Planting" is a story about how an elderly couple, the Hutchensons, deal with the tragic death of their only son. It takes place in the 1920s. Try to **imagine** how the Hutchensons felt upon learning of the death of their son. Think about how it feels to lose a family member. Try to figure out what the Hutchensons might do and say. To help you do this, answer the questions below before you read the story.

1. Have you or someone you know experienced the death of a relative or close friend? If so, what did you do when you first learned of the tragedy?

   _____

2. Why did you react that way?

   _____

Preview the Reading

To preview the story, look at the title and pictures. Where do you think the story takes place?

The Corn Planting

Sherwood Anderson

The farmers who come to our town to trade are a part of the town life. Saturday is the big day. Often the children come to the high school in town.

It is so with Hatch Hutchenson. Although his farm, some three miles from town, is small, it is known to be one of the best-kept and best-worked places in all our section. Hatch is a little gnarled old figure of a man. His place is on the Scratch Gravel Road and there are plenty of poorly kept places out that way.

Hatch's place stands out. The little frame house is always kept painted, the trees in his orchard are whitened with lime halfway up the trunks, and the barn and sheds are in repair, and his fields are always clean-looking.

Hatch is nearly seventy. He got a rather late start in life. His father, who owned the same farm, was a Civil War man and came home badly wounded, so that, although he lived a long time after the war, he couldn't work much. Hatch was the only son and stayed at home, working the place until his father died. Then, when he was nearing fifty, he married a schoolteacher of forty, and they

had a son. The schoolteacher was a small one like Hatch. After they married, they both stuck close to the land. They seemed to fit into their farm life as certain people fit into the clothes they wear. I have noticed something about people who make a go of marriage. They grow more and more alike. They even grow to look alike.

Check-in ▶ Can you imagine what the old couple look like? What their farm is like?

Their one son, Will Hutchenson, was a small but remarkably strong boy. He came to our high school in town and pitched on our town baseball team. He was a fellow always cheerful, bright and alert, and a great favorite with all of us.

For one thing, he began as a young boy to make amusing little drawings. It was a talent. He made drawings of fish and pigs and cows, and they looked like people you knew. I never did know, before, that people could look so much like cows and horses and pigs and fish.

When he had finished in the town high school, Will went to Chicago, where his mother had a cousin living, and he became a student in the Art Institute out there. Another young fellow from our town was also in Chicago. He really went two years before Will did. His name is Hal Weyman, and he was a student at the University of Chicago. After he graduated, he came home and got a job as principal of our high school.

Hal and Will Hutchenson hadn't been close friends before, Hal being several years older than Will, but in Chicago they got together, went together to see plays, and, as Hal later told me, they had a good many long talks.

I got it from Hal that, in Chicago, as at home here when he was a young boy, Will was immediately popular. He was good-looking, so the girls in the art school liked him, and he had a straightforwardness that made him popular with the young fellows.

Hal told me that Will was out to some party nearly every night, and right away he began to sell some of his amusing little drawings and to make money. The drawings were used in advertisements, and he was well paid.

He even began to send some money home. You see, after Hal came back here, he used to go quite often out to the Hutchenson place to see Will's father and mother. He would walk or drive out there in the after-noon or on summer evenings and sit with them. The talk was always of Will.

Check-in ▶ Can you imagine what Hal is like? How does he feel about Will?

Hal said it was touching how much the father and mother depended on their one son, how much they talked about him and dreamed of his future. They had never been people who went about much with the town folks or even with their neighbors. They were of the sort who work all the time, from early morning till late in the evenings, and on moonlight nights, Hal said, and after the little old wife had got the supper, they often went out into the fields and worked again.

You see, by this time old Hatch was nearing seventy and his wife would have been ten years younger. Hal said that whenever he went out to the farm they quit work and came to sit with him. They might be in one of the fields, working together, but when they saw him in the road, they came running. They had got a letter from Will. He wrote every week.

The little old mother would come running following the father. "We got another letter, Mr. Weyman," Hatch would cry, and then his wife, quite breathless, would say the same thing, "Mr. Weyman, we got a letter."

The letter would be brought out at once and read aloud. Hal said the letters were always delicious. Will larded them with little sketches. There were humorous drawings of people he had seen or been with, rivers of automobiles on Michigan Avenue in Chicago, a policeman at a street

crossing, young stenographers hurrying into office buildings. Neither of the old people had ever been to the city and they were curious and eager. They wanted the drawings explained, and Hal said they were like two children wanting to know every little detail Hal could remember about their son's life in the big city. He was always at them to come there on a visit and they would spend hours talking of that.

"Of course," Hatch said, "we couldn't go."

"How could we?" he said. He had been on that one little farm since he was a boy. When he was a young fellow, his father was an invalid and so Hatch had to run things. A farm, if you run it right, is very exacting. You have to fight weeds all the time.

There are the farm animals to take care of. "Who would milk our cows?" Hatch said. The idea of anyone but him or his wife touching one of the Hutchenson cows seemed to hurt him. While he was alive, he didn't want anyone else plowing one of his fields, tending his corn, looking after things about the barn. He felt that way about his farm. It was a thing you couldn't explain, Hal said. He seemed to understand the two old people.

It was a spring night, past midnight, when Hal came to my house and told me the news. In our town we have a night telegraph operator at the railroad station and Hal got a wire. It was really addressed to Hatch Hutchenson, but the operator brought it to Hal. Will Hutchenson was dead, had been killed. It turned out later that he was at a party with some other young fellows and there might have been some drinking. Anyway, the car was wrecked, and Will Hutchenson was killed. The operator wanted Hal to go out and take the message to Hatch and his wife, and Hal wanted me to go along.

I offered to take my car, but Hal said no. "Let's walk out," he said. He wanted to put off the moment, I could see that. So we did walk. It was early spring, and I remember every moment of the silent walk we took, the little leaves just coming on the trees, the little streams we crossed, how the moonlight made the water seem alive. We loitered and loitered, not talking, hating to go on.

Then we got out there, and Hal went to the front door of the farmhouse while I stayed in the road. I heard a dog bark, away off somewhere. I heard a child crying in some distant house. I think that Hal, after he got to the front door of the house, must have stood there for ten minutes, hating to knock.

Then he did knock, and the sound his fist made on the door seemed terrible. It seemed like guns going off. Old Hatch came to the door, and I heard Hal tell him. I know what happened. Hal had been trying, all the way out from town, to think up words to tell the old couple in some gentle way, but when it came to the scratch, he couldn't. He blurted everything right out, right into old Hatch's face.

That was all. Old Hatch didn't say a word. The door was opened, he stood there in the moonlight, wearing a funny long white nightgown, Hal told him, and the door went shut again with a bang, and Hal was left standing there.

He stood for a time, and then came back out into the road to me. "Well," he said, and "Well," I said. We stood in the road looking and listening. There wasn't a sound from the house.

And then—it might have been ten minutes or it might have been a half-hour—we stood silently, listening and watching, not knowing what to do—we couldn't go away—"I guess they are trying to get so they can believe it," Hal whispered to me.

I got his notion all right. The two old people must have thought of their son Will always only in terms of life, never of death.

Check-in ▶ Can you imagine why Hal and the narrator waited; why they couldn't go away?

We stood watching and listening, and then, suddenly, after a long time, Hal touched me on the arm. "Look," he whispered. There were two white-clad figures going from the house to the barn. It turned out, you see, that old Hatch had been plowing that day. He had finished plowing and harrowing a field near the barn.

The two figures went into the barn and presently came out. They went into the field, and Hal and I crept across the farmyard to the barn and got to where we could see what was going on without being seen.

It was an incredible thing. The old man had got a hand corn-planter out of the barn and his wife had got a bag of seed corn, and there, in the moonlight, that night, after they got that news, they were planting corn.

It was a thing to curl your hair—it was so ghostly. They were both in their nightgowns. They would do a row across the field, coming quite close to us as we stood in the shadow of the barn, and then, at the end of each row, they would kneel side by side by the fence and stay silent for a time. The whole thing went on in silence. It was the first time in my life I ever understood something, and I am far from sure now that I can put down what I understood and felt that night—I mean something about the connection between certain people and the earth—a kind of silent cry, down into the earth, of these two old people, putting corn down into the earth. It was as though they were putting death down into the ground that life might grow again—something like that.

They must have been asking something of the earth, too. But what's the use? What they were up to in connection with the life in their field and the lost life in their son is something you can't very well make clear in words. All I know is that Hal and I stood the sight as long as we could, and then we crept away and went back to town, but Hatch Hutchenson and his wife must have got what they were after that night, because Hal told me that when he went out in the morning to see them and to make the arrangements for bringing their dead son home, they were both curiously quiet and Hal thought in command of themselves. Hal said he thought they had got something. "They have their farm and they have still got Will's letters to read," Hal said.

 Final Check-in
Did you imagine the people and places in the story as you read? How did you picture Will? Will's parents?

After You Read

A. Comprehension Check

1. Think about Hatch and his wife. Write two ways they were alike.

   _____

2. Think about Will's personality. Write two or three words that describe him.

   _____

3. Do you think Will would have been happy staying home and becoming a farmer? Explain your answer.

   _____

4. Why didn't Will's parents ever visit him in Chicago?

   _____

5. After Will died, what did his parents have left to comfort them?

   _____

6. When the Hutchensons learned that their son had died, they planted new corn. Why do you think they did this?

   _____

B. Revisit the Reading Strategy Can you imagine how Hal felt when he was asked to deliver the tragic news of Will's death? Imagine how you would have felt. Think about his actions. With a partner or small group, talk about what you might have done.

C. Think beyond the Reading Will wrote to his parents every week. Have you ever tried to maintain a long-distance relationship with a family member or friend? Discuss different ways of keeping in touch with some-one far away. Why is it hard to maintain a long-distance friendship? What can make it worth the effort?

Think About It: Identify Theme

You learned in Lesson 4 that a story's **theme** is its general message about life. Sometimes an author states the theme directly. More often, however, the theme is revealed through the actions and attitudes of the characters, and the events in the plot. In "The Corn Planting," Sherwood Anderson reveals his theme gradually.

A. Look at Theme

This excerpt from "The Corn Planting" indicates the story's theme:

> ▶ It was as though they were putting death down into the ground that life might grow again. . . .

Which of the following sentences comes closest to stating the theme?

1. The theme of the story is "death conquers all in the end."

2. The theme of the story is "affirming life in the face of death."

The second sentence more closely states the theme of "The Corn Planting."

B. Practice Below are several excerpts from "The Corn Planting." Check each one that helps reveal the theme of "affirming life in the face of death."

_____ **1.** ▶ . . . there, in the moonlight, that night, after they got that news, they were planting corn.

_____ **2.** ▶ . . . right away he began to sell some of his amusing little drawings and to make money.

_____ **3.** ▶ What they were up to in connection with the life in their field and the lost life in their son is something you can't very well make clear in words.

_____ **4.** ▶ Hal said it was touching how much the father and mother depended on their one son. . . .

_____ **5.** ▶ They must have been asking something of the earth, too.

▶ **Talk About It**
Discuss couples you know who have a strong relationship and a long marriage like the Hutchensons. Include details that help you picture the couple and their relationship.

Write About It: Write a Friendly Letter

Will Hutchenson wrote to his parents every week. His letters were funny and interesting. Write a letter to a friend or family member you've been meaning to contact.

A. Prewriting Think about what you want to say in your letter. On the lines below, list things you have done recently, people you have talked to, conversations you have had, your feelings about things—anything that will inform or entertain your reader.

Events: _____

People: _____

Conversations: _____

Feelings: _____

B. Writing Write your letter on separate paper. Describe what's happening in your life. Start a new paragraph for each new topic. Use the format of a friendly letter, like the example below.

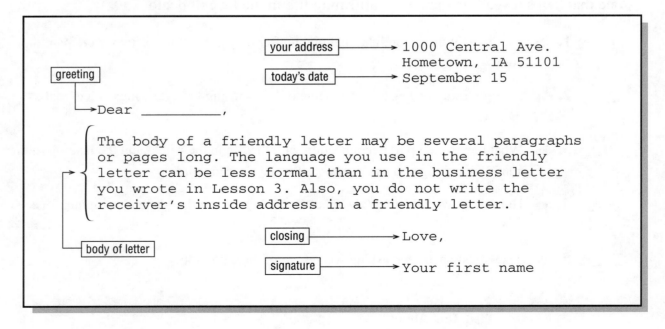

▶ **Save your draft.** At the end of this unit, you will choose one of your drafts to work with further.

Life Skill: Read a Family Tree

A family tree shows several generations. It uses the abbreviations *b.* for born, *m.* for married, and *d.* for died. This example shows two generations from the Hutchenson family tree.

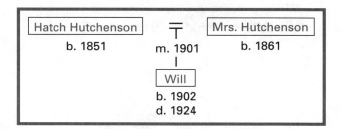

Practice Read the family tree below and answer the questions that follow.

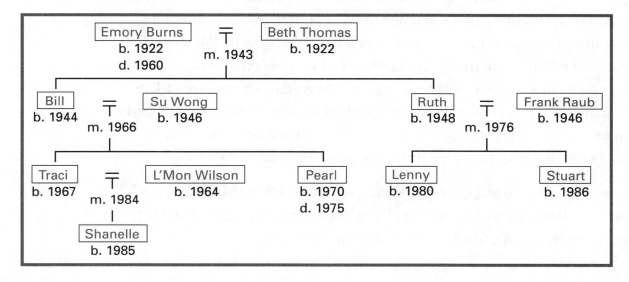

1. When did Beth Thomas marry Emory Burns? _____

2. Who married Ruth Burns? _____

3. How many children did Bill and Su have? _____

4. Who is older, Traci's daughter, Shanelle, or Traci's cousin Stuart? _____

5. Is Lenny's grandfather still alive? _____

6. What is the name of Pearl's uncle? _____

7. What is the name of Stuart's aunt? _____

8. How many first cousins does Traci have? _____

Lesson 9

LEARNING GOALS

Strategy: Use your prior knowledge
Reading: Read a bar graph and a double bar graph
Skill: Identify facts and opinions
Writing: Write your opinion
Life Skill: Read a double line graph

Before You Read

The families in both "On Golden Pond" and "The Corn Planting" included a married couple and one son or daughter. For many years, it was fairly typical for a U.S. household to include a married couple and their children. Households with two parents and one or two children are less common today than in the past. In this lesson, you will read graphs that describe some of the changes in living arrangements and family relationships that have taken place in the U.S. The first graph shows data on the size of U.S. households in 1995. Data is factual information usually expressed in numbers. The second graph compares data on the living arrangements of children who do not live with both parents for the years 1970 and 1995.

Before you read the graphs, think about your **prior knowledge** of recent trends in marriage, divorce, and family relationships. On the lines below, write three things you already know about these topics.

_____

_____

_____

Preview the Reading

Preview the two graphs to get a general idea about the information they present. Read the titles of the graphs and the labels.

 Use the Strategy

As you read the graphs, keep in mind what you already know about living arrangements in the U.S. Does the information in the graphs confirm what you already know?

Recent Trends in U.S. Living Arrangements

Bar Graph for Size of Households

A **bar graph** uses bars of different lengths to show information. Bar graphs are often useful for making comparisons. This bar graph shows the number of households of various sizes in the United States in 1995. The labels under the bars indicate the number of people in a household. The figures along the left side indicate the number of households, in thousands.

To read the graph, look at a bar. For one-person households, the bar goes up to the number 25,000. The actual value is about 25,000 multiplied by 1,000, or 25,000,000 (25 million). So in 1995 there were almost 25 million one-person households in the U.S.

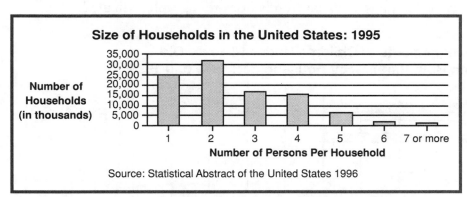

Size of Households in the United States: 1995

Number of Households (in thousands)

Number of Persons Per Household

Source: Statistical Abstract of the United States 1996

What size household was most common in 1995? About how many households had four people? What relationship do you see between size and number of households?

The most common household size was two people. About 15,000,000 households had four people. The more people there are in a household, the fewer households are in that group.

Did your prior knowledge help you to understand the information displayed in this graph?

◀ **Check-in**

Comparing Data with a Double Bar Graph

A **double bar graph** uses bars of different lengths and markings to show comparisons. In this example, a double bar graph is used to compare information for separate years. The U.S. Census Bureau has collected information that shows that the percentage of children under 18 living with both parents has declined in recent years. In 1970, 85 percent of children under 18 were living with both parents. By 1995, that figure had dropped to 69 percent. The **double bar graph** shows who the remaining children lived with for both 1970 and 1995.

The **key** beside the graph tells us that a light bar indicates data for the year 1970 and a dark bar indicates data for 1995. The labels along the bottom indicate the percentage of the total number of children under 18. The labels along the left side indicate who headed up the households.

Look at the comparisons shown by the double bar graph. What percent of children lived in a household headed by a divorced mother in 1970? In 1995? Which two household types showed very little change? What trends does this graph indicate?

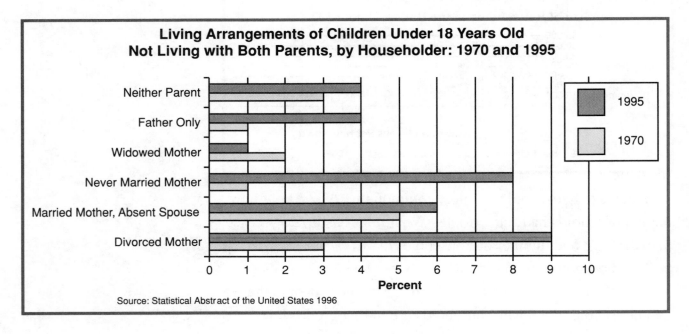

Living Arrangements of Children Under 18 Years Old Not Living with Both Parents, by Householder: 1970 and 1995

Source: Statistical Abstract of the United States 1996

▶ **Final Check-in**

Did the information in the graphs surprise you? Did your prior knowledge help you understand them? Did you learn anything new?

After You Read

A. Comprehension Check

1. About how many four-person households were there in 1995?
   (1) 1,500
   (2) 15,000
   (3) 150,000
   (4) 15 million

2. The single bar graph indicates that, in general, as the size of the household increased, the number of households
   (1) decreased
   (2) increased
   (3) remained the same
   (4) grew larger

3. Which group of householders experienced the largest percent increase of children under 18 living with them?
   (1) widowed mothers
   (2) fathers only
   (3) never married mothers
   (4) divorced mothers

4. Percentages of children under 18 not living with both parents increased in all householder categories except
   (1) fathers only
   (2) neither parent
   (3) divorced mothers
   (4) widowed mothers

B. Revisit the Reading Strategy
Think about what you already knew about households and the relationships among people who live in them. What new information did you learn from the graphs? Discuss with a partner ways in which children are affected by the people who live in their household.

C. Think beyond the Reading
Think about these questions and discuss them with a partner or small group. Answer the questions in writing if you wish.
- Besides the impact on children, what are some other ways that rising divorce rates have affected people's lives and relationships?
- The largest percent change in children's living arrangements occurred in the category of never-married mothers. Discuss some social changes that occurred between 1970 and 1995 that may help explain that increase.

Think About It: Identify Facts and Opinions

The graphs on pages 99 and 100 gave facts about size of households and living arrangements. People can hold strong opinions about these subjects as well. As you learned in Lesson 2, a **fact** is a statement that can be shown to be true, and an **opinion** is a statement of belief, a guess, or a prediction.

People often use facts as a springboard for their own opinions. One person might look at the single bar graph and say, "Look at all the people who are living alone. I think the economy must be doing well if so many people can afford to live by themselves." Another person might look at the same graph and say, "Isn't it sad that so many people live by themselves. A lot of people must be lonely. We should be doing more for them."

Phrases like "I think," "I feel," and "we should" are clues that someone is stating an opinion. But opinion statements do not always contain phrases like "I think." Statements such as "Isn't it sad that so many people live by themselves" and "A lot of people must be lonely" are also opinions.

A. Look at Facts and Opinions

To decide whether a statement is a fact or an opinion, ask yourself: Can it be shown to be true? If it can, it's a fact.

Which of the statements below are facts? Which are opinions?
- The number of children under 18 living in one-parent households increased steadily between 1970 and 1995.
- Most children who are not living with both parents are living with their mothers.
- Only a few children under 18 are living with just their fathers.
- I think that is because the court system is slanted in favor of mothers.

The first three sentences state facts, and the last sentence states an opinion.

B. Practice Each statement below has to do with one of the bar graphs. Write
F for fact or **O** for opinion next to each one.

Single Bar Graph

_____ 1. The greatest number of households in the United States in 1995 consisted of two people.

_____ 2. People who do not live alone are not lonely.

_____ 3. The smallest number of households in the United States in 1995 had seven or more people living in them.

_____ 4. There are about twice as many two-person households as there are four-person households.

_____ 5. Probably most three-person households are made up of a mother and her two children.

Double Bar Graph

_____ 6. In 1970, 85 percent of children under 18 were living with both parents.

_____ 7. Married people got along better in the 1970s than they do now.

_____ 8. The second largest percent increase between 1970 and 1995 occurred in households headed by divorced mothers.

_____ 9. Married mothers whose husbands are absent might as well get a divorce.

_____ 10. Women who aren't married should think twice before having children.

_____ 11. In 1995 more married mothers did not live with their husbands because their husbands were abusive.

_____ 12. A greater percentage of children lived only with their fathers in 1995 than in 1970.

 Talk About It

People often have strong opinions about topics like politics, religion, or lifestyle. People often end up arguing about them. Think about times when you've argued with someone about such a topic. Discuss the following questions with a partner.

- Do you enjoy arguing with some people about politics, religion, or lifestyle?
- Are there some people that you don't enjoy arguing with about these topics? Who are these people? Why don't you like to argue with them?
- Have you ever changed someone's mind about politics, religion, or lifestyle? If so, whose? Why is it usually hard to change someone's mind about these topics?

Write About It: Write Your Opinion

The graphs on pages 99 and 100 provide some interesting information about relationship issues. In this activity, you will have a chance to give your own opinion on one of these issues.

A. **Prewriting** Choose a topic that pertains to relationships. Make sure you have an opinion on this topic. Then brainstorm some ideas about your topic. You can use information from the graphs and draw on your own knowledge and experiences. Then write a sentence stating your opinion on the topic you chose. Finally, list reasons to support your opinion. One way to organize your thoughts is shown below.

Topic: _Divorce is hard on children._

My Opinion: _Married couples should try to stay together for the sake of the children._

Reasons that Support My Opinion

1. _The children of a broken marriage suffer a lot._

2. _Divorce often leads to a lower economic status for the mother and the children. Many divorced mothers with children live in poverty._

3. _When parents divorce, children often feel rejected. They blame themselves for the divorce._

Make your own organizer that includes your topic, your opinion about your topic, and your supporting reasons.

B. **Writing** Write a paragraph that expresses your opinion and supports it with the reasons you listed. First write a topic sentence that states your opinion. Then use the reasons from your organizer to back up your opinion. Add details or examples to explain your reasons.

▶ **Save your draft.** At the end of this unit, you will choose one of your drafts to work with further.

Life Skill: Read a Double Line Graph

A **double line graph,** like a double bar graph, shows similarities and differences between two sets of data. The double line graph below shows U.S. marriage and divorce rates for five-year intervals from 1960 through 1994. Study the graph and answer the questions that follow.

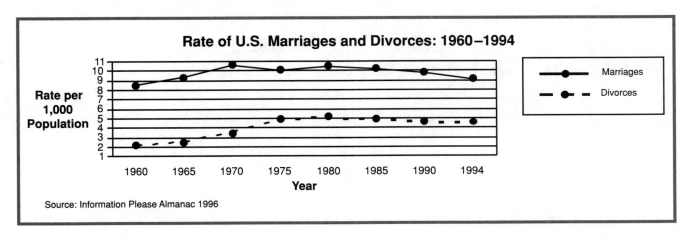

Practice Answer the questions.

1. Per 1,000 people, about how many people got married in 1960?
   (1) 2   (2) 4.5   (3) 6   (4) 8.5

2. Per 1,000 people, about how many people got divorced in 1960?
   (1) 2   (2) 4.5   (3) 6   (4) 8.5

3. Per 1,000 people, about how many people got married in 1985?
   (1) 6   (2) 8   (3) 10   (4) 12

4. In what year was the marriage rate the highest? The lowest? _____

5. In what year was the divorce rate the highest? The lowest? _____

6. What year shows the greatest difference between the marriage and divorce rates? _____

7. What year shows the least difference between the marriage and divorce rates? _____

8. If the general trends in the marriage and divorce rates continue, do you think the divorce rate will ever be greater than the marriage rate? Why or why not?

_____

_____

▶ Writing Skills Mini-Lesson: Writing Complex Sentences

A **complex sentence** has two parts, each with its own subject and verb:

S V   S V

I knew all the other employees when I worked at Pizza World.

independent   dependent
clause   clause

In the sentence above, the first part is the **independent clause.** It is a complete thought and can stand alone. The second part is the **dependent clause.** It begins with the connecting word *when* and cannot stand alone as a separate sentence. Here are some rules for writing complex sentences.

1. **You can begin the sentence with either the independent clause or the dependent clause.**
   - If you put the independent clause first, do not put a comma after it.
     I knew all the other employees when I worked at Pizza World.
   - If you put the dependent clause first, put a comma after it.
     When I worked at Pizza World, I knew all the other employees.

2. **The words below are commonly used in complex sentences. Some connecting words have more than one use.**

Connecting words	Use
before, after, when, while, as, since, as soon as, by the time	time
if, unless	condition
because, since	cause and effect
although, even though, while	contrast

Practice On separate paper, copy each complex sentence, adding a logical connecting word from the chart above. Add a comma when necessary. Then write the sentence another way as in 1 above.

1. I liked working at Pizza World _____ I had a lot of friends there.
2. _____ I was working there the other workers seemed like family.
3. _____ the pay wasn't very good I enjoyed working there.
4. Employees are happier _____ managers treat them well.

Unit 3 Review

Reading Review

Bob the Baby-sitter

"Bob," Lori began. "I'm starting night classes next month, and I was wondering if you could watch Joey on Tuesday and Thursday nights?"

Her ex-husband set down his coffee cup with a resounding crash. "That's the reason you invited me over, to use me as a baby-sitter?"

"For starters," she said, "you're his father. You're not a baby-sitter any more than I am. I'm just asking you for three hours of your time, twice a week."

Bob rolled his eyes. "Why can't your mother do it?"

"Because I'll be going straight from work to night classes. I won't have time to take Joey to her place." Lori stirred her coffee angrily.

"What's in it for me?" Bob asked.

"How about dollar signs?" she said sarcastically.

"Huh?" Now she had his undivided attention.

"Look, if I go back for my high school diploma, I can get a better job, and then you can cut back on child support," Lori said. "Just a little," she added hastily.

Bob sipped his coffee slowly. *He's going to mess with my mind,* she thought. *He'll pretend he's considering it, and then just when I get my hopes up, he'll say no.* She bit her lip to keep from begging.

Just then the front door slammed. Joey ran in, shedding his gym bag. "Dad! Mom!" he yelled. "Watch this." He began kicking his soccer ball through the legs of the kitchen chairs.

"Over here," Bob said, "kick it to me."

"If I let you play soccer, do we have a deal?" Lori asked.

"OK," said Bob. "I'll baby-sit. For now."

Choose the best answer to each question.

1. Which statement is a fact?
   (1) Lori asked Bob for help with child care.
   (2) Bob is not a very dependable person.
   (3) Lori is too trusting.
   (4) Bob drives Lori crazy.

2. Which statement is an opinion?
   (1) Lori and Bob have been divorced for three years.
   (2) Joey is on a soccer team.
   (3) Lori wants to get a better job.
   (4) Lori expects too much from her ex-husband.

3. What is the theme of "Bob the Baby-sitter"?
   (1) Love is better the second time around.
   (2) With age comes wisdom.
   (3) People can cooperate for the sake of their kids.
   (4) Never trust your ex.

4. What can you infer from the statement: "She bit her lip to keep from begging"?
   (1) Lori was good at begging for things.
   (2) Lori didn't want Bob to know how much it meant to her.
   (3) Bob didn't like her to beg.
   (4) Lori's lip was bleeding.

Writing Process

In Unit 3, you wrote three first drafts. Choose the piece that you would like to work with further. You will revise, edit, and make a final copy of this draft.

_____ your dialogue (page 86)

_____ your letter to a friend or relative (page 96)

_____ your opinion about a relationship issue (page 104)

Find the first draft of your choice. Then turn to page 159 in this book. Follow steps 3, 4, and 5 in the Writing Process to create a final draft.

As you revise, check your draft for these specific points:

Dialogue: Make sure the language sounds natural when spoken aloud.

Friendly letter: Make sure the letter is less formal than a business letter.

Opinion paragraph: Be sure it has a topic sentence that states your opinion, and reasons that support it.

Unit 4 Insights

Have you ever been in a situation when something that had confused you suddenly made sense? All at once you understood something that had puzzled you before. Perhaps you had an argument and you suddenly saw the situation from the other point of view. Or you had been puzzled about a math process and suddenly you understood how to do it. If so, you have had a sudden insight.

Insights give you the ability to understand problems or situations. Some develop gradually, as you puzzle over a problem or work your way through an unfamiliar situation. Other insights happen suddenly. A sudden insight feels as if you've turned on a light in a dark room. Before you begin Unit 4, think of an insight you have had. What was the insight? How did it affect you?

▶ **Be an Active Reader**

As you read the selections in this unit

- Put a question mark (?) by things you do not understand.
- <u>Underline</u> words you do not know. Try to use context clues to figure them out.

After you read each selection in this unit

- Reread sections you marked with a question mark (?). If they still do not make sense, discuss them with a partner or your instructor.
- Look at words you <u>underlined</u>. Discuss any words you still don't understand with a partner or your instructor, or look them up in a dictionary.

Lesson 10

LEARNING GOALS

Strategy: Imagine
Reading: Read an autobiography
Skill: Make inferences
Writing: Write the results of an interview
Life Skill: Read a time line

Before You Read

The story in this lesson is from the autobiography of Helen Keller. An autobiography is a real person's life story written by that person. Helen Keller lost her sight and hearing, due to illness, before she was two years old. Since she could neither hear nor see, she didn't know words existed.

Keller described herself as a "wild" child until she was almost seven, when a remarkable teacher came into her life. That teacher, Anne Sullivan, gave Keller the gift of language.

Before you read, **imagine** what it might be like if you had no language for communicating. Think about what kinds of things you would need to communicate. Imagine how you would communicate these things to other people. How would you let someone know you were hungry, cold, hurt, or in trouble? On the lines below, write how you think you would feel and what you would do.

_____

_____

_____

_____

Preview the Reading

To preview this reading from *The Story of My Life,* read the first paragraph and look at the picture on page 113. What part of Helen Keller's life will you be reading about in this excerpt?

▶ **Use the Strategy**
In this selection, Helen Keller describes the events that led to her most important insight after she met her teacher, Anne Sullivan. As you read, imagine yourself in young Helen's place. How do her senses lead her to understand what words are?

from The Story of My Life

Helen Keller

The most important day I remember in all my life is the one on which my teacher, Anne Mansfield Sullivan, came to me. I am filled with wonder when I consider the immeasurable contrasts between the two lives which it connects. It was the third of March, 1887, three months before I was seven years old.

On the afternoon of that eventful day, I stood on the porch, dumb,[1] expectant. I guessed vaguely from my mother's signs and from the hurrying to and fro in the house that something unusual was about to happen, so I went to the door and waited on the steps. The afternoon sun penetrated the mass of honeysuckle that covered the porch, and fell on my upturned face. My fingers lingered almost unconsciously on the familiar leaves and blossoms which had just come forth to greet the sweet Southern spring. I did not know what the future held of marvel or surprise for me. Anger and bitterness had preyed upon me continually for weeks and a deep languor[2] had succeeded[3] this passionate struggle.

Helen Keller at age 74

ASSOCIATED PRESS/WIDE WORLD PHOTOS

Check-in ▶ Why do you think Helen had felt angry and bitter? Imagine how you would have felt in her place.

Have you ever been at sea in a dense fog, when it seemed as if a tangible white darkness shut you in, and the great ship, tense and anxious, groped her way toward the shore with plummet and sounding-line,[4] and you waited with beating heart for something to happen?

---

1. **dumb:** unable to speak.
2. **languor:** tiredness, weakness.
3. **succeeded:** followed.
4. **plummet and sounding-line:** tools used on a ship to measure the water depth.

I was like that ship before my education began, only I was without compass or sounding-line, and had no way of knowing how near the harbor was. "Light! give me light!" was the wordless cry of my soul, and the light of love shone on me that very hour. I felt approaching footsteps. I stretched out my hand as I supposed to my mother. Someone took it, and I was caught up and held close in the arms of her who had come to reveal all things to me, and, more than all things else, to love me.

The morning after my teacher came she led me into her room and gave me a doll. The little blind children at the Perkins Institution had sent it and Laura Bridgman[5] had dressed it; but I did not know this until afterward. When I had played with it a little while, Miss Sullivan slowly spelled into my hand the word "d-o-l-l." I was at once interested in this finger play and tried to imitate it. When I finally succeeded in making the letters correctly I was flushed with childish pleasure and pride. Running downstairs to my mother I held up my hand and made the letters for doll. I did not know that I was spelling a word or even that words existed; I was simply making my fingers go in monkey-like imitation. In the days that followed I learned to spell in this uncomprehending way a great many words, among them *pin, hat, cup,* and a few verbs like *sit, stand,* and *walk.* But my teacher had been with me several weeks before I understood that everything has a name.

◄ Check-in

If you couldn't see or hear, how would you know that words exist? Try to imagine what it would be like not to know what words are.

One day, while I was playing with my new doll, Miss Sullivan put my big rag doll into my lap also, spelled "d-o-l-l" and tried to make me understand that "d-o-l-l" applied to both.

---

5. Laura Bridgman: an educator; the first blind and deaf person to be systematically educated.

Earlier in the day we had had a tussle over the words "m-u-g" and "w-a-t-e-r." Miss Sullivan had tried to impress it upon me that "m-u-g" is *mug* and that "w-a-t-e-r" is *water*, but I persisted in confounding[6] the two. In despair she had dropped the subject for the time, only to renew it at the first opportunity. I became impatient at her repeated attempts and, seizing the new doll, I dashed it upon the floor. I was keenly delighted when I felt the fragments of the broken doll at my feet. Neither sorrow nor regret followed my passionate outburst. I had not loved the doll. In the still, dark world in which I lived there was no strong sentiment or tenderness. I felt my teacher sweep the fragments to one side of the hearth, and I had a sense of satisfaction that the cause of my discomfort was removed. She brought me my hat, and I knew I was going out into the warm sunshine. This thought, if a wordless sensation may be called a thought, made me hop and skip with pleasure.

Anne Bancroft plays Anne Sullivan and Patty Duke plays Helen Keller in the 1962 movie *The Miracle Worker.*

We walked down the path to the well-house, attracted by the fragrance of the honeysuckle with which it was covered. Someone was drawing water and my teacher placed my hand under the

---

6. **confounding:** confusing.

spout. As the cool stream gushed over one hand she spelled into the other the word *water,* first slowly, then rapidly. I stood still, my whole attention fixed upon the motions of her fingers. Suddenly I felt a misty consciousness as of something forgotten—a thrill of returning thought; and somehow the mystery of language was revealed to me. I knew then that "w-a-t-e-r" meant the wonderful cool something that was flowing over my hand. That living word awakened my soul, gave it light, hope, joy, set it free! There were barriers still, it is true, but barriers that could in time be swept away.

I left the well-house eager to learn. Everything had a name, and each name gave birth to a new thought. As we returned to the house every object which I touched seemed to quiver with life. That was because I saw everything with the strange, new sight that had come to me. On entering the door I remembered the doll I had broken. I felt my way to the hearth and picked up the pieces. I tried vainly[7] to put them together. Then my eyes filled with tears; for I realized what I had done, and for the first time I felt repentance and sorrow.

I learned a great many new words that day. I do not remember what they all were; but I do know that *mother, father, sister, teacher* were among them—words that were to make the world blossom for me, "like Aaron's rod, with flowers."[8] It would have been difficult to find a happier child than I was as I lay in my crib at the close of that eventful day and lived over the joys it had brought me, and for the first time longed for a new day to come.

---

7. vainly: without success.
8. This is a reference to Numbers 17 in the Bible.

▶ **Final Check-in**
Can you imagine the joy and excitement Helen felt when she suddenly understood what words are? How do you think her senses of touch and smell helped her understand the meaning of words?

After You Read

A. Comprehension Check

1. Helen Keller writes that the day she met Anne Sullivan was
   (1) a cold winter day
   (2) the most important day of her life
   (3) the day she was forced to grow up
   (4) the day she learned that everything has a name

2. Why was Helen such an angry child before she met Anne Sullivan?
   (1) She was cut off from the world because she was deaf and blind.
   (2) She was given too many toys and was spoiled by her parents.
   (3) Nobody would pay attention to her.
   (4) She was in a dense fog.

3. When Helen realized what *water* meant,
   (1) she was suddenly able to see
   (2) water became more important than anything else to her
   (3) words were easier to spell
   (4) the mystery of language was revealed

4. Why was Anne Sullivan so important in Helen Keller's life?
   (1) Anne taught her and loved her.
   (2) Anne was fun to be with.
   (3) Helen wanted a companion so she wouldn't be lonely.
   (4) Helen wanted to be a teacher.

B. Revisit the Reading Strategy

Imagine yourself as Helen Keller. How would you feel when you made the connection between the liquid on your hand and the word *water?* Check the words that would describe your feelings.

_____ excited   _____ sad   _____ proud   _____ angry   _____ surprised

C. Think beyond the Reading

Think about these questions and discuss them with a partner. Answer them in writing if you wish.

- Can you remember a time, either in school or out, when something that had puzzled or confused you suddenly made sense? How did that make you feel?
- Can you think of a time when you helped someone else have a sudden insight and understand something new? How did you feel then?

Think About It: Make Inferences

In Lesson 7, you learned that you **make inferences** when you read a story and understand more than what is stated in words.

A. Look at Making Inferences

Making inferences is sometimes called "reading between the lines."

What can you infer about Helen from the clues in the passage below?

> ▶ I had not loved the doll. In the still, dark world in which I lived there was no strong sentiment or tenderness.

You can infer that not being able to see or hear had made Helen unable to form emotional attachments.

B. Practice Read the passages below and answer the questions. Use your knowledge of the whole story.

1. ▶ I felt approaching footsteps. I stretched out my hand as I supposed to my mother. Someone took it, and I was caught up and held close in the arms of her who had come to reveal all things to me, and, more than all things else, to love me.

   From this excerpt you can infer that when she wrote this, Helen felt
   (1) confused by meeting a stranger
   (2) sorry for herself
   (3) gratitude and love for her teacher
   (4) surprised that her mother wasn't there

2. ▶ It would have been difficult to find a happier child than I was as I lay in my crib at the close of that eventful day and lived over the joys it had brought me, and for the first time longed for a new day to come.

   You can infer from this that until that day, Helen
   (1) had been a happy child
   (2) had led an unhappy life
   (3) had brought other people joy
   (4) had looked forward to each new day

3. ▶ I was at once interested in this finger play and tried to imitate it. When I finally succeeded in making the letters correctly I was flushed with childish pleasure and pride. Running downstairs to my mother I held up my hand and made the letters for doll. I did not know that I was spelling a word or even that words existed; I was simply making my fingers go in monkey-like imitation.

From this excerpt, you can infer that Helen
(1) was eager to learn new things
(2) knew how to spell most words
(3) was too full of pride
(4) was quick to imitate sounds

4. ▶ Everything had a name, and each name gave birth to a new thought. As we returned to the house every object which I touched seemed to quiver with life. That was because I saw everything with the strange, new sight that had come to me. On entering the door I remembered the doll I had broken. I . . . picked up the pieces. I tried vainly to put them together. Then my eyes filled with tears; for I realized what I had done, and for the first time I felt repentance and sorrow.

a. Why did objects now seem to "quiver with life"? _____

_____

b. What was the "strange, new sight" that Helen had? _____

_____

c. How does Helen's attitude toward breaking the doll change after she understands

language? _____

_____

▶ **Talk About It**
With a partner, discuss what it would have been like to be Helen Keller's parents after her illness left her blind and deaf. How would they have felt? How would they have treated Helen? What plans would they have made?

Write About It: Write the Results of an Interview

Helen Keller's autobiography describes an insight, a moment when she suddenly understood something. One minute she didn't know that words existed. The next minute she had unlocked the mystery of language. Insights happen in many different kinds of situations. In this activity you will write about an insight someone you know had.

A. **Prewriting** Interview someone about an insight he or she has had. Ask questions about the insight and record the answers. You may use the following questions. Add others if you wish. If you can't find anyone to interview, write about an insight you have had yourself.

   1. Describe the situation or problem the insight helped you understand.
   2. How long had you tried to understand it before you had the insight?
   3. What led to the insight?
   4. What was your insight?
   5. How did the situation change as a result of your insight?

B. **Writing** Write a paragraph that explains the person's insight. Start with a topic sentence that states the insight as a main idea. *For example:* Tom had an insight that helped him to understand his fear of the water.

   Then write details about the experience, using the information you gathered in the interview. Write at least one sentence for each answer that you got.

▶ **Save your draft.** At the end of this unit, you will choose one of your drafts to work with further.

Life Skill: Read a Time Line

A **time line** is a graphic way to show when specific events happened. A time line of Helen Keller's early life might include these events:

The time line below shows some events in Helen Keller's later life.

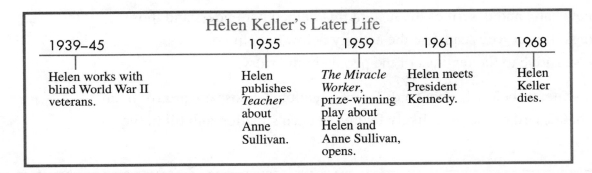

Practice Study both time lines. Then answer these questions.

1. When did illness destroy Helen Keller's sight and hearing? _____

2. How old was Helen when she learned to read braille? _____

3. How old was she when she published her first autobiography? _____

4. When did Helen Keller graduate from Radcliffe College? _____

5. What did Helen Keller do between 1939 and 1945?

_____

6. When did she publish *Teacher*? _____

7. How old was Helen Keller when she died? _____

Lesson 11

LEARNING GOALS

Strategy: Empathize with others
Reading: Read a personal account
Skill: Compare and contrast
Writing: Compare and contrast two things
Life Skill: Fill in a hospital admission form

Before You Read

"A Fear I Had" is a personal account written by Zoraida Pesante [zor AY da pe SAN tay] when she was a student at The Open Book in Brooklyn, New York. In this account, Pesante tells how she had negative feelings about her new baby and describes the insight that helped her understand those feelings. Before you read, use the activity below to help you **empathize,** or be sensitive to the feelings of the people in the story.

Each sentence below is about a different situation. Choose a word from the box that describes the most likely feeling in each situation and fill in the blank.

excited	disappointed	exhausted	proud

1. After working 12 hours straight, Rosa was _____.

2. When Roger won a trip to Spain, he was _____.

3. Miho mastered her new computer program and felt _____.

4. When Joel didn't win the science prize, he felt _____.

Preview the Reading

Preview the story by reading the title and looking at the pictures. Predict what you think the author is afraid of.

A Fear I Had

Zoraida Pesante

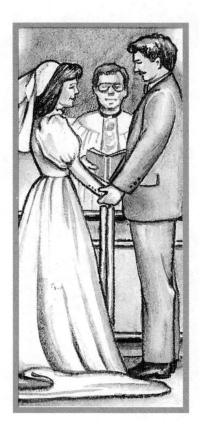

When my fiancé and I got married, we wanted a child, but I had this fear. Would I be a good mother? Could I protect my child from danger? Would he or she feel safe with me? Four years into my marriage I got pregnant. I was afraid it would be a girl. I didn't want a girl. I prayed to God to give me a boy. Then our son was born. I was elated. My prayers were answered. He was my joy. I took care of him like he was the only thing in this world. I watched every move he made. I felt a love for this boy that I couldn't describe. My husband was a little jealous, because I was not paying any attention to him.

When my son was 13 months old, I got pregnant again. I was so mad because I only wanted one child. When I was about three months pregnant, my doctor told me that the baby's heart beat was going very fast and that meant that it's a girl. I felt that she was lying to me because she knew I had a son. How could she tell with just the heart beat? I went home and told my husband that it was going to be a boy. My husband predicted that it will be a girl and that she would be born early. Well, through the whole eight months I kept telling everybody I was going to have a boy. My doctor gave me a sonogram in my eighth month. When the sonogram was over, I was curious to find out what it was. My doctor said that she didn't see anything hanging between the legs. I went home so upset, but I still said it was going to be a boy.

◀ Check-in

The day came for me to go to the hospital to have the baby. I was three weeks early. I was so nervous. My husband left me in the room and he went downstairs to register me at the front desk. While he was there, the receptionist asked him, "Didn't you just bring in your wife?" and he said "yes." She said, "Well, the computer says that your wife just had a girl." He was so happy that he started to cry.

Can you experience Zoraida's feelings for her baby boy? Can you feel as she felt about being pregnant again?

It took me five minutes to have her. I was alone with the nurse. She didn't have time to bring me into the delivery room. The first thing I said when I saw her was, "Oh she is ugly! Put her back!" I brought her home three days later. To everyone that came by to visit us, I would say how ugly she was. I wanted to understand why I was feeling like that toward my daughter. I wanted to know why I didn't love her the same way I loved my son when he was born.

When I was young, I was so naive. I couldn't understand a lot of things that were going on in my life. One of the things that I couldn't understand was that I was sexually abused by two members of my own family. I didn't talk to anybody about this problem until I was in my thirties. I went through a lot when I was young; I felt as I was growing up that only girls go through pain in their life. Then I realized why I was afraid to have a girl. I didn't want her to go through the same pain I did. I didn't want her to experience what I experienced in my life. I didn't want history to repeat itself with her.

▶ Final Check-in
Did you empathize with Zoraida when she thought her baby was ugly?
Did you empathize with her after you found out about her childhood?
Why or why not?

After You Read

A. Comprehension Check

1. How many children did Zoraida want? _____

2. How did she feel about her son? _____

_____

3. How did Zoraida feel about her second pregnancy? _____

_____

4. How did she feel about her baby girl? _____

_____

5. How did Zoraida's husband feel about their baby girl? _____

_____

6. What insight made Zoraida understand why she didn't want to have a girl? _____

_____

7. Do you think her fear was justified? Why or why not? _____

_____

B. Revisit the Reading Strategy Put yourself in Zoraida's place to answer these questions.
   - Can you understand why she didn't talk to anyone about what had happened to her as a little girl?
   - Could you understand her fear about having a daughter after reading about the abuse? Why or why not?
   - Would you have felt the same if a similar thing had happened to you?

C. Think beyond the Reading Think about these questions and discuss them with a partner. Answer them in writing if you wish.

Do you think Zoraida learned to love her daughter? How might she have overcome her initial feelings toward her daughter? What do you think should be done about people who sexually abuse children?

Think About It: Compare and Contrast

In "A Fear I Had," Zoraida describes her and her husband's feelings toward their children. One way to think about their feelings is to compare and contrast them. In Lesson 5, you learned that **comparing** two things means looking for ways they are alike. **Contrasting** them means noticing the ways they are different.

A. Look at Comparing and Contrasting

The chart below compares and contrasts Zoraida's and her husband's desire to have children. For comparisons, information is listed in the column headed **Both**. Contrasting information is listed under each person's name.

How the Pesantes Felt about Children

Topic	Zoraida	Mr. Pesante	Both
Wanted children?			wanted a child when they married
Boy or girl?	wanted only a boy	wanted a boy or a girl	

Comparison: When they got married, both Zoraida and her husband wanted a child.

Contrast: Zoraida wanted only a boy, but her husband wanted either a boy or a girl.

B. Practice

1. Compare and contrast Zoraida with mothers you know. Fill in the missing parts of the chart below.

Compare and Contrast Zoraida and Mothers You Know

Topic	Zoraida	Mothers You Know	Both
Wants children?			yes
Boy or girl?	wants a boy	want _____ _____	
Loves her children?	Loves _____ _____	Love all their children.	

2. Fill in the similarities and differences between Zoraida's son and her daughter in this chart. Write comparisons under **Both.** Write contrasts in the **Son** and **Daughter** columns.

Compare and Contrast Zoraida's Son and Daughter

Topic	Son	Daughter	Both
Parents			
Birth order			
Zoraida's feelings about pregnancy			
Zoraida's feelings at child's birth			
Mr. Pesante's feelings at child's birth			
What Zoraida said about baby			

▶ **Talk About It**

Discuss the following questions in a small group. If a child told you that he or she had been sexually abused, what steps would you take to help? What if the child had been beaten instead of sexually molested? What if the child had been neglected and didn't have proper food or clothing? Should a child be kept with his or her parents no matter what, or are there times when a child would be better off in a different situation?

Write About It: Compare and Contrast Two Things

In "A Fear I Had" Zoraida Pesante describes the very different feelings she had toward her two children when each was born. Those feelings were compared and contrasted earlier in the lesson. In this activity, you will write about the similarities and differences between two things in your own life.

A. **Prewriting** Choose a subject, such as jobs, sports, relatives, or places you've lived. Think of two examples within your subject that you can compare and contrast. Next create a chart like the one below and fill in the similarities and differences between the two things.

Compare and Contrast: Jobs

Topic	Waiting tables	Detailing cars	Both
Co-workers			nice, friendly
Customers	deal with customers	no customer contact	
Wages			low, minimum wage
Extra money	earn tips	no extra money	
Atmosphere	noisy	quiet	

B. **Writing** Follow the steps below to write about the information from your chart. You can write everything in one paragraph or you can write four paragraphs.

1. Give some background on your subject.

2. Write a sentence like: "There are several similarities between two jobs I have had." Include at least one sentence explaining each similarity.

3. Describe the differences, or contrasts, between the two things.

4. Write a closing statement that draws a conclusion about the similarities or differences between the two.

▶ **Save your draft.** At the end of this unit, you will choose one of your drafts to work with further.

Life Skill: Fill In a Hospital Admission Form

When Zoraida Pesante had her second baby, her husband probably had to fill in her hospital admission form. A **hospital admission form** gives the hospital staff the information they need to care for you and to file insurance claims. Read the sample admission form below.

Park Central Medical Center Admission Form

Date _____

Patient Name _____ Phone _____

Address _____

Legal Next of Kin _____ Phone _____

Referring Physician _____

Patient's Employer _____

Patient's Occupation _____ Social Security # _____

Patient's Age _____ Birthdate _____ Sex _____ Marital Status_____

Religion (optional) _____

Method of Payment _____

Insurer's Name and Address _____

Name of Insured_____ Relationship to Patient _____

Policy Number _____ Type of Plan (Group or Individual) _____ .

Patient's Medical History

List previous illnesses/accidents and dates.

List previous hospital stays and dates.

Any allergies?   Yes   No   (If yes, specify.)

I, the patient or responsible person, will assume financial responsibility for all room accommodations occupied and all charges incurred while hospitalized.

_____ Date _____
(signature)

Practice Fill out the admission form as if you were entering the hospital.

Lesson 12

LEARNING GOALS

Strategy: Use your prior experience
Reading: Read a biographical article
Skill: Understand cause and effect chains
Writing: Write a cause and effect paragraph
Life Skill: Read a circle graph

Before You Read

In this lesson, you will read "A Success as a Teacher and Builder, John Corcoran Had a Humiliating Secret: He Couldn't Read or Write." You will learn how Corcoran hid the fact that he could not read. In this article, he also explains how and why he finally did learn to read. He describes the moment of insight when words on a page made sense for the first time.

Before you read, use your own **prior experience** to help you understand Corcoran's situation. Think about skills you have mastered, either as a child or in your adult life. They might be skills like cutting hair, repairing a carburetor, or in-line skating. (Even skills that are fun have to be learned.) On the lines below, list some of the skills you have mastered.

_____   _____

_____   _____

Preview the Reading

To preview the article, first read the title. Does it make you curious? Do the words *success* and *humiliating secret* seem to contradict each other?

▶ **Use the Strategy**

In this article, John Corcoran describes the tricks he used to keep people from finding out he couldn't read. He also talks about why he finally decided, at age 48, to learn to read and how he accomplished it. As you read, use your prior experience to understand his struggle.

A Success as a Teacher and Builder

John Corcoran Had a Humiliating Secret: He Couldn't Read or Write

*Brad Darrach
and Dianna Waggoner*

Corcoran gestures in triumph at his declaration of independence, but for 40 years he couldn't spell even a three-letter word.

Success sat on Big John Corcoran like antlers on a bull elk. Six-foot-four and built like a fullback, he sported a mop of gray-blond hair, a speaking voice that played bass fiddle on a listener's bones, and ice-blue eyes that lit up like headlights when he switched on the charm. With energy, presence and a flair for the dramatic, he survived college and graduate school, became a respected social studies teacher in Oceanside, Calif., then turned a $2,500 investment into a house-building business employing more than 200 people. At 48, Corcoran was a multimillionaire who owned a $600,000 villa with a slam-dunk view of the Pacific, went off on European vacations with his attractive wife, Kathy—and lived in terror that somebody might expose his unspeakable secret: He was a total illiterate.

"Reading," he now admits, "was to me like looking at Chinese, at scribbles. I couldn't get the letters and the words together. And the higher I climbed, the harder it became to expose myself, to ask for help. They'd have thrown me out of college if they'd known, and who would employ an illiterate teacher? I was trapped. If the truth got out, how could I support my family? So my life turned into a nightmare. For 40 years I lived like a fugitive. There was no day I didn't dread that someone would find me out."

Incredibly, nobody did. But two years ago Corcoran finally turned himself in. He showed up at an adult learning center, asked for help and got it. Now literate at last, he has taken to the lecture circuit, where his cautionary tales have awakened thousands to the horrors of illiteracy—while offering them at the same time all the chills and thrills of hearing a man with one leg tell how he climbed Mount Everest.

How did Corcoran fool all of the people all of the time? At first he didn't. His elementary school teachers in various towns in the Southwest knew he couldn't read. But instead of testing him for a learning disability,[1] they just figured he was lazy, rebellious or stupid and passed him along to the next grade. Perhaps if he had stayed in one school long enough, a teacher might have found a way to help him. But his family moved too often: In 12 years John attended 17 schools.

His parents were equally undiscerning.[2] "John, where was I?" his mother, Agnes, asked in stricken amazement when the oldest of her six children at last unloaded his burden. "Raising five other kids, Ma," he replied gently. And why didn't his father, John, a high school business teacher, sense the problem? Possibly because he was too busy moving from town to town in search of a better job.

---

1. learning disability: a physical or psychological cause for difficulty in learning.
2. undiscerning: lacking insight.

Have you experienced teachers or parents who completely overlooked a problem like John Corcoran's? How do you think he felt as he slipped further and further behind?

Cheating helped Corcoran slither through high school in Blythe, Calif., and the University of Texas at El Paso. He often signed up for too many classes, then dropped those requiring too much writing. He persuaded his girlfriends to write compositions for him, and during exams arranged to sit beside good students and laboriously copy their work.

When he couldn't cheat, Corcoran sweated blood. In college it took him five days of drudgery[3] to memorize the letters that stand for the 96 chemical elements, and after passing the test he cried himself to sleep. "There was no way," he remembers thinking, "that I was ever going to get out of this." But he did. "I learned from radio, TV, film. I picked people's brains. People were my library."

The pressure eased in graduate school, where oral and take-home exams were common. Corcoran won four National Science Foundation grants and pulled an A in sociology at the University of Santa Clara. But when he decided to teach ("After all I'd been through, I really felt I had something to offer my students"), he had to conjure up a whole new bag of tricks. Bookkeeping classes were no problem—he was a whiz with numbers—but when he taught social studies, he assigned no written homework, gave no written tests and never used the blackboard. Pupils chose up sides and debated the subject—in effect, they taught themselves. Corcoran brought in outside speakers. His classes churned with energy and surprises, and students loved them. "A lot of good learning took place," says his former principal. "John was a very good teacher."

Business confronted Corcoran with another set of challenges. In his checkbook he kept a list of spelled-out numbers, and he always asked the people he paid to fill in their own names. No big deal having lunch with a client: He just waved the menu aside and asked for whatever popped into his head. But what about the dozens of letters, memos and contracts that crossed his desk every

---

3. drudgery: hard, dull work.

day? Corcoran developed preemptive strategies:[4] "*You* read it," he would tell his secretary. "I left my glasses at home." Or: "I'm too busy. Give me a summary." With a sigh, he says, "I had a hundred excuses."

As for contracts, he brought them home to be vetted[5] by his wife, and he took her along when he had to sign papers at the bank. Kathy was the only living soul who knew his secret. He had confessed it to her before they were married, but she hadn't believed him. "I thought he meant he didn't read *well*," she says. For several years, she avoided the issue. Then one day she heard him pretending to read a nursery tale to his baby daughter. In fact, he was simply making up a story that fit the pictures. "My God!" she realized. "He *really* can't read."

Kathy now admits that living with an illiterate can be almost as stressful as being one. "We got into arguments over me having to write things. But when I said, 'Look it up!' his eyes were like he wanted to kill me, because he didn't even know the first letter." Why didn't she teach him to read? "I sensed that it was something he didn't want to deal with, that I would only be adding to his fear and frustration."

Decades of fear and frustration cut deep scars into Corcoran's basic good nature. "He became an angry, fearful man," Kathy says. "Fearful of being exposed, of feeling dumb and unworthy." Corcoran agrees: "I acted angry, but I really felt frightened and ashamed. If you came close to me, you came close to my secret and you were a danger, even if your intentions were friendly." As a result, the Corcorans made few friends. They had their children, Colleen, 22, and John, 19, and they had each other. But there were times when they were terribly lonely in their palace by the sea.

◀ Check-in

Have you known anyone who used strategies similar to John Corcoran's to hide the fact that they couldn't do something?

It took a severe shock—the collapse of his business when the California building boom went bust in 1982—to persuade Corcoran to face his problem. Stripped of the staff that had served

---

4. preemptive strategies: moves made to prevent something else from happening.
5. vetted: examined expertly.

as his word processor, he felt "like a quarterback without blockers or receivers," he says. So after rescuing his business, he took steps to rescue himself—wary steps. Still fearful that neither the public nor the banks would support any business run by an illiterate, he withheld the name of his company from Lynda Jones, director of the regional adult learning program.

"It was so hard," Corcoran says of their first meeting. "I don't even know how the words came out. But I said, 'I can't read at all.'" To test the accuracy of this claim, Jones asked Corcoran to write a few sentences stating what he hoped to gain from the literacy program. "It was awful," he says. "Trying to do something children can do, and failing." In frustration he clutched his pencil like a knife and began stabbing the page.

Jones put Corcoran in touch with a volunteer tutor named Eleanor Condit, and the two of them hit it off from the first. "I was like a little boy talking to his third-grade teacher," he recalls, his eyes misting with emotion. "He was so eager," says Condit. "I sensed that here was a man with unlimited ability. But the tools had never been there." They met twice a week in a local firehouse, and Corcoran spent 40 to 60 hours a week doing homework.

"The first 30 days," Corcoran says, "it was touch and go. I couldn't make connections. But suddenly a bell rang—BING!" Words emerged where there had only been infuriating squiggles. "So that's how you look!" Corcoran found himself murmuring. Words were no longer his enemies. The whole world became a friendlier place—and Corcoran a friendlier man. "A healing has gone on in him that is just incredible," says Kathy.

What's more, Corcoran's fears of a public backlash have proved groundless. Business is booming and associates are warmly supportive. Some say he is living proof that literacy is overrated. But to that he gives an unanswerable answer: "Who would want one eye when he can have two?"

Corcoran can now read to his granddaughter, Kayla.

PEOPLE WEEKLY ©1988 Tony Korody

▶ **Final Check-in**

Have you ever had to work as hard to learn something as John Corcoran worked at learning to read? How did your prior experience help you to better understand Corcoran's struggle?

After You Read

A. Comprehension Check

1. John Corcoran lived in fear that
   (1) his business would collapse
   (2) people would find out he couldn't read
   (3) his wife would leave him
   (4) his students would do badly

2. Corcoran could be described as
   (1) lazy
   (2) determined
   (3) unmotivated
   (4) shy

3. Corcoran realized he had to learn to read when
   (1) he started to teach
   (2) he was in college
   (3) his business collapsed
   (4) his granddaughter was born

4. When Corcoran had his insight,
   (1) squiggles became words
   (2) he hadn't studied at all
   (3) words became his enemies
   (4) he got new eyeglasses

B. Revisit the Reading Strategy Based on your prior experience, do you agree with the following statements?

Yes	No	Maybe	
_____	_____	_____	1. Reading is the basis for success in life.
_____	_____	_____	2. Learning a new skill requires determination.
_____	_____	_____	3. Learning any new skill is easy.

C. Think beyond the Reading Think about these questions and discuss them with a partner. Answer them in writing if you wish.

1. John Corcoran's inability to read and write led him to do things he knew were wrong, such as cheat to get through school. How do you think these actions made him feel about himself? Why?

2. Do you think it's possible to help insights happen? If so, how?

Think About It: Understand Cause-and-Effect Chains

You learned in Lesson 1 that a **cause** is the reason why something happens. The **effect** is what happens—the result or outcome of the cause. Often in a story the effect of one action becomes the cause of the next action. When this happens, the events are part of a **cause-and-effect chain.**

A. Look at Cause-and-Effect Chains

Read this sentence from the article and fill in the missing elements in the diagram below.

▶ It took a severe shock—the collapse of his business when the California building boom went bust in 1982—to persuade Corcoran to face his problem.

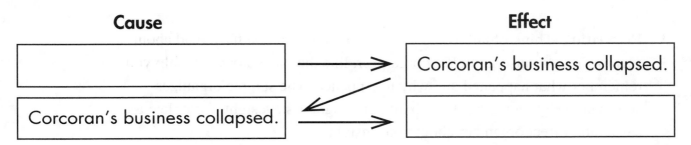

Cause   **Effect**

	Corcoran's business collapsed.
Corcoran's business collapsed.	

The missing cause was that the California building boom went bust. The missing effect was that Corcoran was persuaded to face his problem.

B. Practice Read the excerpt and fill in the diagram.

▶ Words were no longer his enemies. The whole world became a friendlier place—and Corcoran a friendlier man.

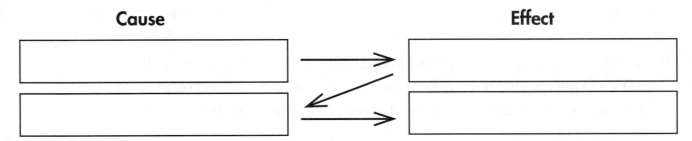

Cause   **Effect**

▶ Talk About It

John Corcoran reads to his granddaughter now. Form a group of four or five people. Take turns telling fairy tales or other stories. Tell stories that you read to children now or remember from your own childhood.

Write About It: Write a Cause-and-Effect Paragraph

The article about John Corcoran describes the moment of sudden insight when words began to make sense to him. Notice that it took him a month of studying full-time to achieve this insight:

> ▶ "The first 30 days," Corcoran says, "it was touch and go. I couldn't make connections. But suddenly a bell rang—BING!" Words emerged where there had only been infuriating squiggles.

You have probably had a sudden insight. Perhaps you suddenly understood another person's point of view. Or maybe you finally thought of a solution to a problem that had been troubling you. In this activity, you will write about your insight.

A. Prewriting Think of an insight you have had or one you have read about or seen on TV. A cause-and-effect organizer, like the one below, can help you remember what happened and why it happened. The sample organizer shows an insight a mother had about her daughter's eyesight. Complete a cause-and-effect organizer about your insight.

Insight: How I Recognized My Daughter's Problem

Cause	Effect
✦ In 5th grade, my daughter's grades suddenly fell; she had always done well in school. ⟶	✦ We were all worried. We couldn't figure out what was wrong.
✦ One day I asked her to tell me the time by looking at the big clock on the kitchen wall. She couldn't read it. ⟶	✦ I suddenly realized she needed glasses. I was relieved.
✦ We got glasses for her. ⟶	✦ Her grades improved rapidly.

B. Writing Write a paragraph about your insight. Describe the situation that led up to the insight. Tell what the insight was and how it made you feel. Be sure to explain the details by using the causes and effects in the organizer you filled in.

▶ **Save your draft.** At the end of this unit, you will choose one of your drafts to work with further.

Life Skill: Read a Circle Graph

In Lessons 3, 6, and 9 you learned how to read bar graphs and line graphs. Another kind of graph is a **circle graph,** also called a **pie chart.** The circle represents 100 percent of something, such as the total money in a budget or all the people in a group. Each section of the circle stands for a part of the whole circle. The size of each section depends upon what percent of the total that part of the whole makes up. As with any graph, it's important to read the title and labels to understand what each section represents.

The circle graph below shows how many years of school people age 25 and older had completed by 1995. The section labels tell the various levels of school completed. Notice that the size of each section reflects the percentage it represents. The percentages must add up to 100 percent. All of the percentages are based on a total of 166,438,000 people.

Practice Study the circle graph. Then answer the questions.

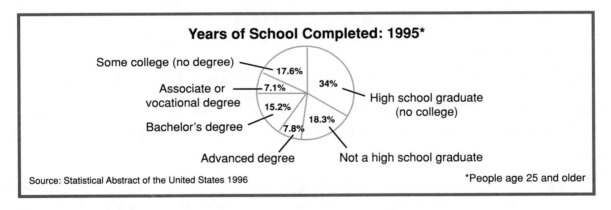

1. What does this circle graph show? _____

2. What is the largest single group on the graph? _____

3. What percentage of people age 25 or older had not completed high school in 1995? _____

4. Which group is larger, those with a bachelor's degree or those with an advanced degree?

_____

5. What total percentage never attended college? _____

6. What total percentage have attended some college or earned a degree beyond high school?

_____

▶ Writing Skills Mini-Lesson: Correcting Pronoun Problems

A **pronoun** is a word that takes the place of a noun. In the examples below, the pronouns *she* and *her* take the place of the noun *mother.*

My **mother** had a hard life. I didn't understand my **mother.**

⬇   ⬇

She had a hard life.   I didn't understand **her.**

She is a **subject pronoun,** and *her* is an **object pronoun.**

1. **Use a subject pronoun in the subject position of a sentence.** A subject pronoun tells who or what is doing the action of the verb. A subject pronoun usually comes before the verb.

   Subject pronouns are *I, you, he, she, it, we, they.*
       She was always tired. **I** didn't understand. **We** didn't help.

2. **Use an object pronoun in the object position of a sentence.** An object pronoun usually comes after a verb or after a preposition (such as to, for, or with). It tells who or what receives the action of the verb.

   Object pronouns are *me, you, him, her, it, us, them.*
       My mother helped **me.** I loved **her.** She did everything for **us.**

3. **Errors often occur when two pronouns or a noun and a pronoun are joined by the word *and*.** These are called compound pronouns. If the compound is in the subject position, use subject pronouns. If the compound is in the object position, use object pronouns.

Right	Wrong
He and I didn't help.	**Him and me** didn't help.
My mother talked to **her and me.**	My mother talked to **she and I.**
She helped **Tom and me.**	She helped **Tom and I.**

Practice Copy the sentences, choosing the correct pronouns from the choices.

1. (I, me) _____ didn't understand my mother and often got mad at (she, her) _____.
2. (She, Her) _____ was always tired and seldom played with (we, us) _____ kids.
3. Then (I, me) _____ had children, and I began to understand (she, her) _____.
4. Both (she and I, her and me) _____ raised our children and worked full-time.
5. I understood why mother had so little time for (Tom and I, Tom and me) _____.

Unit 4 Review

Reading Review

The Wheelchair Adventurer

Janet Lee James was 22 years old when she was diagnosed with multiple sclerosis (MS), a disease that attacks the body's nerves. She had just graduated from college and gotten a job at an advertising agency when, she says, she "began to sense that something strange was going on inside my body."

When James realized how severe her illness was, she knew she had better hurry up and live life. MS is the biggest crippler of young adults, and although she didn't have many symptoms, she knew it was just a matter of time. First on her agenda was to pursue her dream of being a disc jockey. She worked at a radio station for a year, always aware that her body was degenerating. Then her best friend moved away, and one night James began screaming, "I gotta go. I gotta go." Two weeks later she arrived in Anchorage, Alaska, thousands of miles from her friends, her family, and her past.

"Everything fell into place," she recalls. "A twenty-three-year-old lunatic with an incurable disease can fly to Alaska and everything can work out. There was no fear, nothing but excitement."

The MS attacks came and went, and most of the time they hardly slowed her down. James hiked, fished, climbed glaciers, learned to sail, drove a dogsled, and experimented with hot-air ballooning, scuba diving, and whitewater rafting. "I lived for adventure," she says. "Nobody ever had a better time or did more exotic, strange things than I did in an eight-year period."

Inevitably, however, the day came when she was so incapacitated that she had to return to Pittsburgh, her hometown. There, she began reliving her adventures by writing a book about them. Her book, called *One Particular Harbor,* was published in 1993.

Choose the best answer to each question.

1. You can infer that Janet James is
   (1) timid
   (2) adventurous
   (3) unmotivated
   (4) a quitter

2. For James, fighting MS is like
   (1) being a disc jockey
   (2) going crazy
   (3) working in advertising
   (4) conquering glaciers and rivers

3. James decided to hurry up and live because
   (1) she was diagnosed with MS
   (2) she didn't like her job
   (3) she was afraid of the wilderness
   (4) her best friend moved away

4. What insight led James to go to Alaska?
   (1) She felt that she had an illness.
   (2) She had a boring job.
   (3) She had limited time for adventure.
   (4) Her illness made it hard to do things.

Writing Process

In Unit 4, you wrote three first drafts. Choose the piece that you would like
to work with further. You will revise, edit, and make a final copy of this
draft.

_____ your interview about an insight (page 118)

_____ your comparison and contrast of two things in your own life (page 126)

_____ your cause-and-effect paragraph of an insight that you have had (page 136)

Find the first draft of your choice. Then turn to page 159 in this book.
Follow steps 3, 4, and 5 in the Writing Process to create a final draft.

As you revise, check your draft for these specific points:

Results of an interview: Make sure you included a topic sentence and
   details that describe the person's insight.

Comparison and contrast: Be sure you explained both the similarities and
   differences.

Cause-and-effect paragraph: Be sure your details include a cause that leads
   to each effect.

Skills Review

This Skills Review will let you see how well you can use the skills taught in this book. When you have finished Units 1–4, complete this review. Then share your work with your instructor.

Reading Skills Review

Read each passage and answer the questions that follow.

The Multicultural Workplace

We have all learned behaviors from the cultures we were raised in. Today, people from different cultures often come into contact at the workplace. When they do, those different behaviors can clash, leading to misunderstandings and even anger. The more we know about other cultures, the more we can avoid such tensions.

Consider this example. Koreans are raised to believe it's rude to touch a person you don't know well, so many Korean shop-keepers don't hand customers their change. Instead, they put it on the counter. But an American customer might think the Korean is avoiding contact out of disgust. The very behavior that is meant to show respect is then seen as disrespectful. Similarly, in many Asian cultures, avoiding eye contact is a sign of respect. A co-worker of European ancestry, however, might interpret it as a sign that the person is lying.

How can misunderstandings like these be avoided? First, don't get angry. Try to put yourself in the other person's place. Think about how you would like to be treated. If you work with or live near people from different cultures, try to learn more about those cultures. When you know why people do certain things, you probably won't get angry anymore.

Choose the best answer to each question.

1. Based on the article, which is correct?
   (1) Europeans avoid eye contact.
   (2) Asians make eye contact out of respect.
   (3) Asians avoid eye contact out of respect, but Europeans may think they are lying.
   (4) Both Europeans and Asians avoid eye contact when they are lying.

2. The last paragraph is about
   (1) how you would like to be treated
   (2) ways to avoid misunderstandings
   (3) why people do certain things
   (4) cultural differences

Deportation at Breakfast

Larry Fondation

The signs on the windows lured me inside. For a dollar I could get two eggs, toast, and potatoes. The place looked better than most—family-run and clean. The signs were hand-lettered and neat. The paper had yellowed some, but the black letters remained bold. A green and white awning was perched over the door, where the name "Clara's" was stenciled.

Inside, the place had an appealing and old-fashioned look. The air smelled fresh and homey, not greasy. The menu was printed on a chalkboard. It was short and to the point. It listed the kinds of toast you could choose from. One entry was erased from the middle of the list. By deduction, I figured it was rye. I didn't want rye toast anyway.

Because I was alone, I sat at the counter, leaving the empty tables free for other customers that might come in. At the time, business was quiet. Only two tables were occupied; and I was alone at the counter. But it was still early—not yet seven-thirty.

Behind the counter was a short man with dark black hair, a mustache, and a youthful beard, one that never grew much past stubble. He was dressed immaculately, all in chef's white—pants, shirt, and apron, but no hat. He had a thick accent. The name "Javier" was stitched on his shirt.

I ordered coffee, and asked for a minute to choose between the breakfast special for a dollar and the cheese omelette for $1.59. I selected the omelette.

The coffee was hot, strong, and fresh. I spread my newspaper on the counter and sipped at the mug as Javier went to the grill to cook my meal.

The eggs were spread out on the griddle, the bread plunged inside the toaster, when the authorities came in. They grabbed Javier quickly and without a word, forcing his hands behind his back. He, too, said nothing. He did not resist, and they shoved him out the door and into their waiting car.

On the grill, my eggs bubbled. I looked around for another employee—maybe out back somewhere, or in the wash room. I leaned over the counter and called for someone. No one answered. I looked behind me toward the tables. Two elderly men sat at one; two elderly women at the other. The two women were talking. The men were reading the paper. They seemed not to have noticed Javier's exit.

I could smell my eggs starting to burn. I wasn't quite sure what to do about it. I thought about Javier and stared at my eggs. After some hesitation, I got up from my red swivel stool and went behind the counter. I grabbed a spare apron, then picked up the spatula and turned my eggs. My toast had popped up, but it was not browned, so I put it down again. While I was cooking, the two elderly women came to the counter and asked to pay. I asked what they had had. They seemed surprised that I didn't remember. I checked the prices on the chalkboard and rang up their order. They paid slowly, fishing through large purses, and went out, leaving me a dollar tip. I took my eggs off the grill and slid them onto a clean plate. My toast had come up. I buttered it and put it on my plate beside my eggs. I put the plate at my spot at the counter, right next to my newspaper.

As I began to come back from behind the counter to my stool, six new customers came through the door. "Can we pull some tables together?" they asked. "We're all one party." I told them yes. Then they ordered six coffees, two decaffeinated.

I thought of telling them I didn't work there. But perhaps they were hungry. I poured their coffee. Their order was simple: six breakfast specials, all with scrambled eggs and wheat toast. I got busy at the grill.

Then the elderly men came to pay. More new customers began arriving. By eight-thirty, I had my hands full. With this kind of business, I couldn't understand why Javier hadn't hired a waitress. Maybe I'd take out a help-wanted ad in the paper tomorrow. I had never been in the restaurant business. There was no way I could run this place alone.

Choose the best answer to each question.

3. Why did the author take over cooking?
   (1) He thought Javier might get in trouble.
   (2) Nobody else noticed the cook was gone.
   (3) He had always wanted to be a cook.
   (4) His eggs were burning.

4. The author kept serving customers because
   (1) he wanted the tips
   (2) he had finished his breakfast
   (3) he thought Javier would be back
   (4) there was no one else to do it

5. Which of the following statements from the story is a fact?
   (1) The place had an appealing and old-fashioned look.
   (2) They seemed not to have noticed Javier's exit.
   (3) There was no way I could run this place alone.
   (4) Then they ordered six coffees.

6. From the title, you can infer that Javier was arrested because he was
   (1) an illegal immigrant
   (2) not paying minimum wages
   (3) not paying his taxes
   (4) a police informant

7. The author started thinking about running the restaurant. From this, you can infer
   (1) he had a good job already
   (2) he didn't know how to cook
   (3) he enjoyed working at the restaurant
   (4) he didn't like dealing with customers

8. Which best states the theme of the story?
   (1) Small actions can sometimes lead to surprising results.
   (2) Taking over something that isn't yours is wrong.
   (3) Helping out can get you into trouble.
   (4) Illegal workers are always caught.

Taking a Stand Against Pollution

Chester is a city in southeastern Pennsylvania. In 1989, the richest county in the state began shipping its garbage to Chester to be burned. Every day, 2,600 tons of burning garbage polluted the town. The air smelled terrible. Soot caked people's windows, and red smoke floated across the sky. Children had trouble breathing. The smoke also contained sulfur dioxide, one of the compounds in acid rain.

One woman, Zulene Mayfield, decided to fight back against the polluters. In 1992 she and her neighbor Horace Strand started the Chester Residents Concerned for Quality Living. This grassroots group staged protests and sued the companies that were polluting. In 1994, thanks to the group's activities, the city council passed the nation's first local zoning law against new industries that pollute. However, pollution from industries that were in operation prior to the law's passage remains a problem.

Mayfield works in the suburbs. As she drives to her job, she passes bundles of garbage that will end up in her neighborhood. And she keeps on fighting.

People all over the country are joining the fight to provide a cleaner environment. When a lot of people take a stand against pollution, it can add up to a big difference. The graph below shows how much two kinds of air pollution declined between 1970 and 1994.

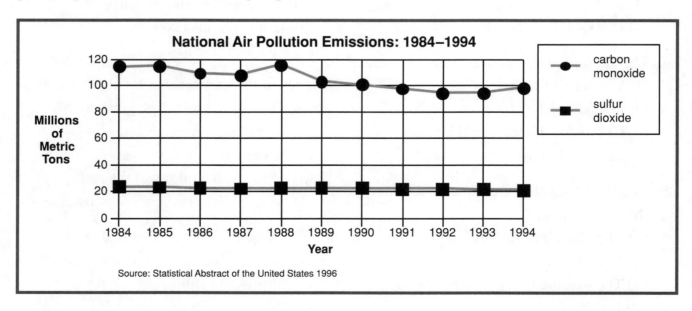

National Air Pollution Emissions: 1984–1994

Source: Statistical Abstract of the United States 1996

Choose the best answer to each question.

9. It's an opinion that
(1) Zulene Mayfield took a stand against air pollution in her city
(2) officials probably would not have put an incinerator in the suburbs
(3) the Chester residents' group sued polluting companies
(4) garbage from Chester's suburbs is trucked into the city to be burned

10. What is the main idea of the graph?
(1) Carbon monoxide and sulfur dioxide are two types of air pollution.
(2) Carbon monoxide emissions increased between 1987 and 1988.
(3) Sulfur dioxide emissions are measured in metric tons.
(4) Overall, both types of emissions have decreased from 1984 to 1994.

Writing Skills Review

Copy the paragraph and edit it. Correct errors in subject-verb agreement, compound and complex sentences, and pronoun use.

I dated a girl named Hannah, when I was 16 years old. Her and me was very close. Hannah loved to read books. Once I asked Hannah for a date but she wanted to finish reading a book instead! At first I were angry. Then Hannah started talking about the book so I listened to the story. The book was about Captain Ahab and a white whale. After the whale bit off Ahab's leg the captain tried to catch and kill the whale. He hunted the whale for years. The story sounded stupid to I. Then late one night Hannah and me was watching an old movie on TV called *Moby Dick*. We watched Captain Ahab stalk the whale and I finally understood the story. It weren't stupid at all.

Write About It

On a separate piece of paper, write about the topic below. Then use the Revising Checklist to revise your draft.

Topic Do you think that people are lonelier today than they used to be? Why or why not? Write one or more paragraphs to explain your opinion.

Revising Checklist

Revise your draft. Check that your draft
_____ clearly states your opinion
_____ includes reasons to support your opinion
_____ includes details or examples to explain your reasons

Skills Review Answers

Reading Skills Review

1. (3)	**6.** (1)
2. (2)	**7.** (3)
3. (4)	**8.** (1)
4. (4)	**9.** (2)
5. (4)	**10.** (4)

Writing Skills Review

I dated a girl named Hannah when I was 16 years old. **She** and **I were** very close. Hannah loved to read books. Once I asked Hannah for a date, but she wanted to finish reading a book instead! At first I **was** angry. Then Hannah started talking about the book**, so** I listened to the story. The book was about Captain Ahab and a white whale. After the whale bit off Ahab's leg**,** the captain tried to catch and kill the whale. He hunted the whale for years. The story sounded stupid to **me.** Then late one night Hannah and **I were** watching an old movie on TV called *Moby Dick.* We watched Captain Ahab stalk the whale**,** and I finally understood the story. It **wasn't** stupid at all.

Write About It

Make changes on your first draft to improve your writing. Then recopy your draft and share it with your instructor.

▶ **Student Self-Assessment** Go on to page 148 to complete Student Self-Assessment #2.

Evaluation Chart

Check your Skills Review answers. Then, on the chart below, circle the number of any answer you missed. You may need to review the lessons indicated next to that question number.

Question	Skill	Lessons
1	compare and contrast	5, 11
2	identify the main idea	3, 6
3	understand cause and effect	1, 12
4	understand cause and effect	1, 12
5	identify facts and opinions	2, 9
6	make inferences	7, 10
7	make inferences	7, 10
8	identify theme	4, 8
9	identify facts and opinions	2, 9
10	identify the main idea	3, 6

Student Self-Assessment #2

After you have completed the units in *Voyager 6*, answer these questions.
With your instructor, compare these answers to your answers on Student
Self-Assessment #1. Note any areas in which you have shown progress.

Reading	Good at this	Improving	Little progress
I can read and understand			
1. stories, poems, biographies, fables, and essays			
2. articles in magazines, newspapers, books, and letters			
3. paycheck stubs, forms, and applications			
4. charts, graphs, diagrams, maps, and time lines			
5. political cartoons			
When I read, I can			
1. figure out new words by using context clues			
2. empathize with characters in a story			
3. use what I already know to help me understand			
4. skim to get a general idea of the reading material			
5. try to predict what is coming next			
6. visualize what I read			
7. identify cause and effect relationships			
8. identify facts and opinions			
9. identify the main idea, details, and theme			
10. compare and contrast information			
11. make inferences about information not stated			
12. summarize what I've read			

Writing	Good at this	Improving	Little progress
I can fill in or write			
1. paragraphs with a topic sentence and supporting details			
2. forms and applications			
3. business and friendly letters			
4. stories, biographical sketches, and dialogue			
5. my opinion on an issue			
6. an article based on comparisons and contrasts			
7. an article based on cause and effect			
When I write, I can			
1. think of good ideas and organize them			
2. use facts, examples, or reasons to support my main ideas			
3. express myself clearly so others understand			
4. revise my writing to improve it			
5. edit my writing to make subjects and verbs agree			
6. write and punctuate compound and complex sentences correctly			
7. use the correct forms of pronouns			

Answer Key

When sample answers are given, your answers may use different wording but should be similar to them.

Unit 1: Success at Work

▼ Lesson 1

Before You Read (p. 14)
Possible answers:
1. George was scared.
2. Tomás was angry.
3. Elisha felt proud.
4. Kate felt under pressure.

After You Read (p. 19)
A. 1. (1)
2. (2)
3. (4)
4. (4)

Think About It: Understand Cause and Effect (p. 20)
B. Practice

Cause	Effect
1. Carmen didn't want to alienate her customers.	She remained courteous and patient.
2. Carmen couldn't tolerate Madeline's attacks.	Carmen suggested Madeline go elsewhere.
3. Carmen believed people stole food only because they were hungry.	Carmen felt sorry for the Dukes.
4. The other customers heard that "spics were buying." Madeline Hannon talked to the other customers.	The customers abandoned the store. The other customers came back.

Life Skill: Read a Paycheck Stub (p. 23)
Practice
1. 32 hours
2. $42.00
3. $25.00
4. yes, 8 hours
5. $180.37

▼ Lesson 2

After You Read (p. 27)
A. 1. (3)
2. (3)
3. (4)
4. (1)
5. Sample answer:
Jill may get fired because she makes mistakes on the cash register, has been late for work, and doesn't seem very interested in her job. She has been warned about coming in late twice.

Think About It: Identify Facts and Opinions (p. 28)
B. Practice
1. F	9. F
2. O	10. O
3. O	11. F
4. F	12. O
5. O	13. F
6. F	14. F
7. F	15. O
8. F	

Life Skill: Fill In a Vacation Request Form (p. 31)
Practice
1. 10 days
2. She will be on vacation 16 days if she includes all three weekends.

▼ Lesson 3

After You Read (p. 37)
A. 1. (4)
2. (1)
3. (4)
4. (1)
B. Sample answers:
1. What the boss expects of you.
2. Avoid talking about personal problems and gossiping.

Think About It: Identify the Main Idea and Details (p. 38)

B. Practice

Sample answers:

1. You need to know your mental strengths and weaknesses
   The details are examples.
2. find a job with salary and benefits that fit your needs
   Schedule, salary, and benefits that don't fit your needs can create stress.
   The details are reasons.
3. Here are some basic commonsense expectations of any job.
   The details are examples.
4. Fay must be able to meet the tough physical demands of her job
   The details are facts.

Life Skill: Another Look at Reading a Bar Graph (p. 41)

Practice

1. salespersons, retail
2. 670,000
3. about 650,000
4. about 500,000
5. by 110%
6. The graph on page 36 shows percentages by which jobs are expected to increase, while the graph on page 41 shows numbers of new jobs in each job category.

▼ Writing Skills Mini-Lesson: Subject-Verb Agreement with *be* and *have* (p. 42)

Practice

I **have** always believed in Marco. Marco is my boyfriend. He **has** a good job as a chef. He **has** been working at the restaurant for two years. Just a few years ago, Marco was out of work. His relatives **were** very worried about him, but I **was** not. I **was** sure he **was** going to find a good job. Now we **are** all happy for Marco.

▼ Unit 1 Review (p. 43)

Reading Review

1. (3)
2. (1)
3. (2)

Unit 2: Taking a Stand

▼ Lesson 4

After You Read (p. 51)

A. 1. (4)
   2. (1)
   3. (2)
   4. (3)

Think About It: Identify Theme (p. 52)

B. Practice

1. Possible answers: He went to Tallahassee and established that the Kissimmee town charter was illegal. He upset the town leaders: the mayor, the chief of police, and the judge. He showed them that, in order to stop him from fighting racism, they would have to kill him. He risked his life for what he believed.
2. Possible answer: is taking great risks when standing up for what is right
3. (3)

Life Skill: Read a Political Cartoon (p. 55)

Practice

Possible answers:

1. the Ku Klux Klan
2. She wants the commission to protect them from the racists.
3. He means that the members of the Civil Rights Commission are also members of the Ku Klux Klan; or He means that racism is everywhere—even in the Civil Rights Commission.
4. Both comment on the Klan's illegal and immoral actions. Both accuse people in power of being racist.

▼ Lesson 5

After You Read (p. 61)

A. Possible answers:

1. for political freedom for her people and the right to own land
2. Her parents and brother had been killed by the military, and she was in danger for speaking out on behalf of the peasants. She left so she could tell the story of her people to the outside world.

3. In 1992
4. Thousands of supporters lined the streets and cheered for her.
5. Thousands of people protesting the military dictatorship were massacred.
6. for democracy and the human rights of the people in her country
7. She was placed under house arrest for leading the struggle for human rights.
8. The military would not allow her to return to her country.

Think About It: Compare and Contrast (p. 62)
B. Practice
The chart might be filled in as follows. Your answers may be different.

Comparison and Contrast of Menchú and Suu Kyi

Topic	Menchú	Suu Kyi	Both
Former colonial ruler	Spain	Britain	
Risks they took			risked her life
What they were resisting			government oppression
What they were fighting for			freedom, democracy
When they won Nobel Peace Prize	1992	1991	

Life Skill: Read a Map (p. 65)
Practice
1. Mexico, Belize, El Salvador, and Honduras
2. the Caribbean Sea
3. the Pacific Ocean

▼ Lesson 6
Check-in (p. 67)
The quotation is from the Declaration of Independence of the United States.

After You Read (p. 69)
A. 1. (2)
   2. (4)
   3. (2)
   4. (3)
B. 1. Agree
   2. Disagree
   3. Disagree

Think About It: Identify the Main Idea and Details (p. 70)
B. Practice
1. Details: be able to work together, to pray together, to struggle together, to go to jail together, to stand up for freedom together The details are examples.
2. a. Let freedom ring across the United States.
   b. All the details are high places in various states.
3. Sample answer: Dr. King had a dream that one day prejudice and racism would no longer exist in the United States.

Life Skill: Read a Line Graph (p. 73)
Practice
1. The graph shows minority members of the U.S. Congress between 1981 and 1995.
2. 17
3. 41
4. They are increasing in number and in percentage of all members of Congress.
5. Asian/Pacific Islanders

▼ Writing Skills Mini-Lesson: Commas in Compound Sentences (p. 74)
Practice
My family always reads and talks about the news. We discuss and even argue about politics. My mother and father have voted in every election since 1968. My brother voted four years ago, but I was too young to vote then. I turned eighteen last year, and I voted for the first time. My sister and I registered to vote on the same day. We all voted in the next election, but we voted for different people. My mother and father voted for the Democratic candidate. My sister and brother voted for the Republican candidate, and I voted for an independent. My candidate lost, but I was still excited about voting for the first time.

▼ Unit 2 Review (p. 75)
Reading Review
1. (2)
2. (3)
3. (4)
4. (4)

Unit 3: Relationships

▼ Lesson 7

After You Read (p. 83)

A. 1. (2)
2. (4)
3. (1)
4. (2)

Think About It: Make Inferences (p. 84)

B. Practice

1. a. You can infer that Ethel loves Chelsea, but she doesn't like Chelsea's negative attitude.
   b. You can infer that Chelsea and Ethel probably weren't very close when Chelsea was growing up.
2. a. You can infer that Chelsea loves her father but hasn't been able to communicate with him. She wants them to be closer.
   b. You can infer that Norman does not feel comfortable talking about feelings, either Chelsea's or his own.

Life Skill: Read a Map (p. 87)

Practice

1. Route 381
2. Interstate Highway 70/76
3. Routes 130 and 381
4. Route 711, U.S. Highway 30, Route 381
5. (3)
6. (2)
7. no

▼ Lesson 8

After You Read (p. 94)

A. Possible answers:

1. They were both small; both loved the farm and worked hard to keep it well tended; both loved Will and treasured Will's letters; both looked forward to Hal's visits.
2. cheerful, fun-loving, talented, amusing, outgoing, creative
3. Will probably would not have been happy staying home. He loved the excitement of city life and he liked drawing better than farming.

4. A farm requires work every day, and they didn't want anyone else caring for their cows or their fields.
5. They had their farm and Will's letters to comfort them.
6. They planted the corn to affirm and honor their son's life; to produce new life in the face of death; to assure themselves that life goes on.

Think About It: Identify Theme (p. 95)

B. Practice

1, 3, and 5 help reveal the theme.

Life Skill: Read a Family Tree (p. 97)

Practice

1. 1943
2. Frank Raub
3. two daughters: Traci and Pearl
4. Shanelle is older (born in 1985; Stuart in 1986).
5. no
6. Uncle Frank (Raub)
7. Aunt Su (Wong)
8. two: Lenny and Stuart

▼ Lesson 9

After You Read (p. 101)

A. 1. (4)
2. (1)
3. (3)
4. (4)

Think About It: Identify Facts and Opinions (p. 102)

B. Practice

1. F	5. O	9. O
2. O	6. F	10. O
3. F	7. O	11. O
4. F	8. F	12. F

Life Skill: Read a Double Line Graph (p. 105)

1. (4)	4. 1970/1960
2. (1)	5. 1980/1960
3. (3)	6. 1970
	7. 1994

8. Possible answers: Yes, the difference between marriage rates and divorce rates has been decreasing in recent years. or No, the divorce and marriage rates increase and decrease in a similar pattern.

▼ Writing Skills Mini-Lesson: Writing Complex Sentences (p. 106)

Practice

In each sentence, more than one connecting word is possible. Here are some suggestions.

1. I liked working at Pizza World because I had a lot of friends there.
   Since I had a lot of friends there, I liked working at Pizza World.
2. While I was working there, the other workers seemed like family.
   The other workers seemed like family when I was working there.
3. Although the pay wasn't very good, I enjoyed working there.
   I enjoyed working there even though the pay wasn't very good.
4. Employees are happier when managers treat them well.
   If managers treat them well, employees are happier.

▼ Unit 3 Review (p. 107)

Reading Review

1. (1)
2. (4)
3. (3)
4. (2)

Unit 4: Insights

▼ Lesson 10

After You Read (p. 115)

A. 1. (2)
   2. (1)
   3. (4)
   4. (1)

Think About It: Make Inferences (p. 116)

B. Practice

1. (3)
2. (2)

3. (1)
4. Possible answers:
   a. Objects now had names. Helen could think about them now that they had names. They became "alive" to her.
   b. the ability to understand what language is about
   c. She feels sad that she destroyed something with meaning.

Life Skill: Read a Time Line (p. 119)

Practice

1. in 1881
2. 10 years old
3. 22 years old
4. in 1904
5. She worked with blind World War II veterans.
6. in 1955
7. 88 years old

▼ Lesson 11

Before You Read (p. 120)

Possible answers:

1. exhausted
2. excited
3. proud
4. disappointed

After You Read (p. 123)

A. 1. one

Possible answers:

2. She loved him a great deal.
3. She was angry because she only wanted one child.
4. She thought the baby was ugly, and she didn't love her as she had her son.
5. He was so happy he started to cry.
6. She remembered that she had been sexually abused when she was young and didn't want her daughter to go through the same experience.

Think About It: Compare and Contrast (p. 124)

B. Practice

1.

Compare and Contrast Zoraida and Mothers You Know

Topic	Zoraida	Mothers You Know	Both
Wants children?			yes
Boy or girl?	wants a boy	want _either a a boy or a girl_	
Loves her children?	Loves _only her son, not her daughter_	Love all their children.	

2. Sample answers:

Compare and Contrast Zoraida's Son and Daughter

Topic	Son	Daughter	Both
Parents			Zoraida and her husband
Birth order	born first	born second	
Zoraida's feelings about pregnancy			worried, afraid she would have a girl
Zoraida's feelings at child's birth	elated, overjoyed	upset, unhappy	
Mr. Pesante's feelings at child's birth	a little jealous	very happy	
What Zoraida said about baby	He was my joy. I was elated. My prayers were answered.	She is ugly. I didn't love her the same way.	

▼ **Lesson 12**

After You Read (p. 134)

A. 1. (2)
   2. (2)
   3. (3)
   4. (1)

Think About It: Understand Cause-and-Effect Chains (p. 135)

B. Practice

Cause	Effect

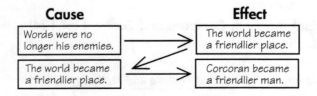

Life Skill: Read a Circle Graph (p. 137)

Practice

1. the years of school completed by people age 25 and over in 1995
2. high school graduates
3. 18.3%
4. those with a bachelor's degree
5. 52.3% (18.3% + 34%)
6. 47.7% (17.6% + 7.1% + 15.2% + 7.8%)

▼ **Writing Skills Mini-Lesson: Correcting Pronoun Problems (p. 138)**

Practice

1. I didn't understand my mother and often got mad at her.
2. She was always tired and seldom played with us kids.
3. Then I had children, and I began to understand her.
4. Both she and I raised our children and worked full-time.
5. I understood why mother had so little time for Tom and me.

▼ **Unit 4 Review (p. 139)**

Reading Review

1. (2)
2. (4)
3. (1)
4. (3)

Writing Skills

This handbook lists the rules you learned in the Writing Skills Mini-Lessons in this book.

Subject-Verb Agreement with *be* and *have*

Every sentence has a **subject** (who or what the sentence is about) and a **verb** (what the subject does or is). The verb can be a single verb. In this case, the single verb is called the **main verb.** The verb may also be a **verb phrase** consisting of a main verb and other verbs, such as *is going* or *have known.* The other verbs in a verb phrase are called **helping verbs.** Both *be* and *have* can be the main verb in a sentence. *Be* and *have* can also be helping verbs. When *be* and *have* stand alone as main verbs or act as helping verbs, they must **agree** with their subjects. Follow these rules:

1. **The present tense of the verb *be* has three forms:** *am, is,* and *are.*

Singular	Plural
I am	we are
you are	you are
he/she/it is	they are

   Used as main verbs: I **am** a sales associate. Steven **is** a nurse. We **are** a team.

   Used as helping verbs: We **are working** in Atlanta. You **are looking** great!

2. **The past tense of *be* has two forms:** *was* and *were.*

Singular	Plural
I was	we were
you were	you were
he/she/it was	they were

   Used as main verbs: He **was** a teacher. My cousins **were** here last week.

   Used as helping verbs: He **was teaching** math. My cousins **were going** home.

3. **The present tense of *have* has two forms:** *have* and *has.*

Singular	Plural
I have	we have
you have	you have
he/she/it has	they have

   Used as main verbs: I **have** a new job. My sister **has** a new job. We both **have** new jobs.

   Used as helping verbs: She **has worked** here for two months. They **have learned** new skills.

   Note: The past tense of *have* has only one form: *had.*

Commas in Compound Sentences

Use a comma to separate the simple sentences in a **compound sentence,** but do not use a comma in a **compound subject** or **compound verb.**

1. **Compound sentences.** A compound sentence has two parts. Each part is a complete thought and has its own subject and verb. You join the two parts with a connecting word like *and, or, but, yet,* or *so.* Use a comma **before** the connecting word.

    Subject   Verb   Subject Verb
    Some people want new leaders, **so** they vote for new candidates.

    Subject   Verb   Subject Verb
    Some people want new leaders, **but** they refuse to vote.

2. **Compound subjects and verbs.** Two subjects joined with the word *and* make a compound subject.

    Compound
    Subject   Verb
    Men and women register before an election.

    Two verbs joined with *and* make a compound verb.

    Subject   Compound
               Verb
    People **go and vote** on election day.

    Do not use a comma before *and* in a compound subject or verb.

Writing Complex Sentences

A **complex sentence** has two parts, each with its own subject and verb:

$$S \quad V \qquad\qquad\qquad S \quad V$$

I knew all the other employees ︸ when I worked at Pizza World.

                independent   dependent

                  clause   clause

In the sentence above, the first part is the **independent clause.** It is a complete thought and can stand alone. The second part is the **dependent clause.** It begins with the connecting word *when* and cannot stand alone as a separate sentence. Here are some rules for writing complex sentences.

1. **You can begin the sentence with either the independent clause or the dependent clause.**

   * If you put the independent clause first, do not put a comma after it.

     I knew all the other employees when I worked at Pizza World.

   * If you put the dependent clause first, put a comma after it.

     When I worked at Pizza World, I knew all the other employees.

2. **The words below are commonly used in complex sentences. Some connecting words have more than one use.**

Connecting words	Use
before, after, when, while, as, since, as soon as, by the time	time
if, unless	condition
because, since	cause and effect
although, even though, while	contrast

Correcting Pronoun Problems

A **pronoun** is a word that takes the place of a noun. In the examples below, the pronouns *she* and *her* take the place of the noun *mother.*

My **mother** had a hard life. I didn't understand my **mother.**

She had a hard life.   I didn't understand **her.**

She is a **subject pronoun,** and *her* is an **object pronoun.**

Subject Pronouns	
I	it
you	we
he/she	they

Object Pronouns	
me	it
you	us
him/her	them

1. **Use a subject pronoun in the subject position of a sentence.** A subject pronoun tells who or what is doing the action of the verb. A subject pronoun usually comes before the verb.

    She was always tired. **I** didn't understand. **We** didn't help.

2. **Use an object pronoun in the object position of a sentence.** An object pronoun usually comes after a verb or after a preposition (such as *to, for,* or *with).* It tells who or what receives the action of the verb.

    My mother helped **me.** I loved **her.** She did everything for **us.**

3. **Errors often occur when two pronouns or a noun and a pronoun are joined by the word** *and.* These are called compound pronouns. If the compound is in the subject position, use subject pronouns. If the compound is in the object position, use object pronouns.

Right	Wrong
He and I didn't help.	**Him and me** didn't help.
My mother talked to **her and me.**	My mother talked to **she and I.**
She helped **Tom and me.**	She helped **Tom and I.**

The Writing Process

The Writing Process is a series of stages that can help you create a good piece of writing. These stages are shown below.

1. Prewrite, or plan your writing.

A. Think about your topic.

B. List ideas about your topic.

C. Organize your ideas.
- Decide which ideas you will use.
- Decide how you will order them.

2. Write a first draft.

A. Use your ideas from stage 1.

B. Write about your topic.
- Clearly state your main ideas.
- Give appropriate facts, examples, or reasons to support your main idea.

3. Revise your first draft.

A. Check that your draft

_____ includes your important ideas

_____ develops the topic with appropriate facts, examples, or reasons

_____ is clear and easy to understand

B. Make changes to improve your writing.
- You can add, cross out, or move information.
- You can reword sentences

4. Edit your work.

A. Check your draft for errors in

_____ complete sentences

_____ correct spelling

_____ correct punctuation

_____ correct capitalization

_____ correct usage

B. Correct any mistakes you find. If you need help, use the Writing Skills Handbook on page 155 or ask your instructor.

5. Recopy your draft.

A. Write a final draft. Include all of your revising and editing changes.

B. Compare your first and final drafts. Note improvements.

C. Share your final draft with a classmate, a friend, or your instructor.